Spiritual Diversity And Social Work

A Comprehensive Bibliography With Annotations

Compiled by

Edward R. Canda, Ph.D.
School of Social Welfare
University of Kansas

Mitsuko Nakashima, M.A., MSW
Ph.D. Student, School of Social Welfare
University of Kansas

Virginia L. Burgess, Ph.D.
Rio Rancho Public Schools
Rio Rancho, New Mexico

Robin Russel, Ph.D.
School of Social Work
University of Nebraska at Omaha

From the Council on Social Work Education's Series

Teaching Social Work:
Resources for Educators

Council on Social Work Education
1600 Duke Street, Suite 300
Alexandria, VA 22314-3421

Printed in the United States of America

Spiritual Diversity and Social Work: A Comprehensive Bibliography with Annotations

Compiled by Edward R. Canda, Mitsuko Nakashima, Virginia L. Burgess, and Robin Russel

ISBN 0-87293-069-6

Table of Contents

Introduction

This bibliography is a comprehensive listing of more than 550 writings on spirituality and social work in the English language. It shows the full range of topics, authors, and opinions that define the state of the art. It is organized according to topics, making it convenient for scholars, students, and practitioners to identify reference materials matching their interests. It also includes 100 brief annotations that highlight a wide range of works within each topic. Anyone who wishes a broad overview of the field can read these 100 items. People researching any particular topic can be assured of a very thorough familiarity with previous work if they read all relevant items.

In keeping with common convention in social work literature, the term spirituality is used to refer to a universal aspect of human experience concerned with the search for a sense of meaning, purpose, and morally satisfying relationships with self, other people, the universe, and ultimate reality, however a person or group understands it (see Canda, 1997, in section D). Therefore, people may express spirituality through participation in religious institutions and traditions (e.g., Christianity or Buddhism) or through philosophical views not limited to any particular religion (e.g., existentialism or transpersonalism). Spirituality also takes on diverse forms in various cultural contexts and social work practice situations. Therefore, entries are classified under subheadings according to the following major topics: religious and non-religious spiritual perspectives; cultural perspectives and issues pertaining to spirituality; spirituality in various fields of social work; general concepts, concerns, and approaches about spirituality and religion; and ethics, values, and moral issues.

Given the large number of entries, we have listed each item only once, even though the topic categories are not mutually exclusive. Each item is placed within the topic category that matches its primary emphasis. However, there are some ways that the reader can identify the relevance of an entry to other categories. Sometimes this is obvious from a title. If the item is annotated, the description will indicate relevance to another category. Also, some topic categories involve a close association with others for many entries. For example, many Buddhist entries are relevant to the Asian and Asian-American cultural issues topic. In turn, many Asian and Asian-American entries are relevant to the religious and nonreligious perspectives topics of Buddhism, Confucianism, Gandhian activism, Hinduism, and Taoism. Common cross-relevancies are indicated with each topic heading.

Methodology for Selection and Annotation of Entries

This bibliography incorporates and expands significantly previous versions prepared by the first author under the auspices of the Society for Spirituality and Social Work (SSSW), published in 1990, 1991, and 1992. The authors thank the SSSW for permission to use these materials.* We thank Cathleen Lewandowski, Ph.D., Department of Social Work, Wichita State University, for her assistance with the 1992 version, and Rebecca Vela, Ph.D. student at the School of Social Welfare, University of Kansas, for her assistance with the present bibliography.

---

* For further information, contact: Robin Russel, Ph.D., Director, Society for Spirituality and Social Work, School of Social Work, University of Nebraska at Omaha, Omaha, NE 68182; (402) 554-2941.

This bibliography includes only entries that are linked directly to social work. Items selected discuss topics related to spirituality in a religious or nonreligious form explicitly, though they need not have used that term. Linkage to social work is determined by one or more of three features of the entry: the author is identified as a social worker; the publication source is a social work journal or book publisher; and the content discusses social work. There are numerous publications on spirituality in allied fields that are relevant to social work. However, these types of items were not included unless social work was discussed in the content.

The four authors collaborated in a process of compiling entries from the previous SSSW bibliographies, their own literature-based research, and computer-assisted searches of *Social Work Abstracts* and *Psychological Abstracts*. These searches were concluded in October 1998. All items identified by these procedures were included. The authors' manual searches also identified many items not included in the two computerized literature databases.

The first author developed the topic categories, made final decisions on classifying entries, selected the 100 items (about 17% of the total) to be annotated, and wrote the annotations with assistance from the co-authors. Each topic category includes some annotated entries. Topic categories with few entries were over-represented in the percentage of annotations, so that these less frequently heard voices on spirituality would not be neglected. In order to compensate, topic categories with many entries, such as Christianity, were under-represented. Within each topic, entries were selected for annotation from a wide range of viewpoints and authors. Entries were also given preference for annotation if they are books, "classic" older works, items widely cited in the field, and if they explicitly address spirituality as a major focus.

The annotations are descriptive. They do not imply endorsement or evaluation of quality for any entry. They briefly identify the topic, methodology, and intent of the author's contribution. In most cases, the annotations were developed by reading the actual publication. In cases of inaccessible material, published abstracts were used.

Suggestions for Seeking Further Information

People who wish to find materials published after this compilation can follow our procedures. When using literature databases, some useful search stems (capital letters removed) are: alcoholics anonymous; buddhis; christian; church; cult; confucian; existential; hindu; islam; jew; judaism; jung; moslem; muslim; religio; sectarian; shaman; spirit; transpersonal; twelve steps; zen. To find spiritual content related to particular cultural groups not defined by religion (e.g., African American), it is helpful to peruse a hard copy of *Social Work Abstracts* using the appropriate ethnic, cultural, or racial terms. Look for abstracts that indicate some treatment of spirituality, even when not indicated explicitly in the title.

It is also fruitful to peruse hard copies of indexes and tables of contents for journals and newsletters that focus on spirituality and social work. These include:
- The Jewish Social Work Forum
- Journal of Jewish Communal Service
- Social Thought: The Journal of Religion in the Social Services
- Social Work and Christianity: An International Journal
- Spirituality and Social Work Newsletter.

A. Religious and Nonreligious Spiritual Perspectives

1. Alternative Religions

Addis, M., Schulman-Miller, J., & Lightman, M. (1984). The cult clinic helps families in crisis. *Social Casework, 65*(9), 515-522.

Bloch, A. C., & Shor, R. (1989). From consultation to therapy in group work with parents of cultists. *Social Casework, 70*(4), 231-236.

Clifford, M. W. (1994). Social work treatment with children, adolescents, and families exposed to religious and Satanic cults. *Social Work in Health Care, 20*(2), 35-59.

Goldberg, L. (1997). A psychoanalytic look at recovered memories, therapists, cult leaders, and undue influence. *Clinical Social Work Journal, 25*(1), 71-86.

> The author states that there has recently been a dramatic increase in recovered memories of sexual abuse, especially within the context of "cults." A psychoanalytic framework is used to discuss this phenomenon and therapeutic responses.

Goldberg, L., & Goldberg, W. (1982). Group work with former cultists. *Social Work, 27,* 165-170.

Lewandowski, C. A., & Canda, E. (1995). A typological model for the assessment of religious groups. *Social Thought: The Journal of Religion in the Social Services, 18*(1), 17-38.

McShane, C. (1993). Satanic sexual abuse: A paradigm. *Affilia, 8*(2), 200-212.

Robbins, S. P. (1995). Cults. In R. L. Edwards (Ed.-in-Chief), *Encyclopedia of Social Work* (19th ed., pp. 667-677). Washington, DC: NASW Press.

> The author provides a detailed critical review of social work and mental health–related literature on "cults." Allegations of widespread abuse and criminal behavior under the influence of alternative religious groups are examined on the basis of empirical research and legal and ethical concerns regarding bias and restrictions on religious freedom.

Wheeler, B. R., Wood, S., & Hatch, R. J. (1988). Assessment and intervention with adolescents involved in Satanism. *Social Work, 33,* 547-550.

2. Buddhism (see also B.2)

Brandon, D. (1976). *Zen in the art of helping.* New York: Delta/Seymour Lawrence.

> The author draws on his social work experience in England, as well as stories and concepts from Zen Buddhist and Taoist traditions, to present a way of helping based on clear awareness, empathy, and spontaneity.

Brandon, D. (1979). Zen practice in social work. In D. Brandon & B. Jordon (Eds.), *Creative Social Work* (pp. 30-35). Oxford, England: Basil Blackwell.

Brenner, M. J. (1997). *To hear and to respond: The influence of Zen Buddhist meditation on the practice of clinical social work.* Unpublished doctoral dissertation, Simmons College.

Canda, E. R., & Phaobtong, T. (1992). Buddhism as a support system for Southeast Asian refugees. *Social Work, 37,* 61-67.

> The authors present results from a qualitative field study of Buddhist mutual assistance associations for Southeast Asian refugee communities in the Midwest. Ideology of service and support systems relating to physical, mental, social, and spiritual needs are described. Implications for culturally appropriate practice are presented.

Compton, J. L. (1982). Sri Lanka's Sarvodaya Shramadana movement: Promoting people's participation in rural community development. *Journal of the Community Development Society, 13*(1), 83-104.

Eppsteiner, F. (Ed.). (1988). *The path of compassion: Writings on socially engaged Buddhism.* Berkeley, CA: Parallax.

Keefe, T. (1975). A Zen perspective on social casework. *Social Casework, 56*(3), 140-144.

Macy, J. (1983). *Dharma and development: Religion as a resource in the Sarvodaya self-help movement.* West Hartford, CT: Kumarian.

Smith, K. (1975). Wholesomeness: Approaches to diagnostic assessment. In T. Tulku (Ed.), *Reflections of mind* (pp. 128-144). Emoryville, CA: Dharma.

3. Confucianism (see also B.2)

Chu, K. F.-Y., & Carew, R. (1990). Confucianism: Its relevance to social work with Chinese people. *Australian Social Work, 43*(3), 3-9.

> The authors present an introduction to Confucianism and its importance to Chinese people. They discuss ways that social work practice with Chinese people can be improved through this knowledge.

Chung, D. (1992). The Confucian model of social transformation. In S. M. Furuto et al. (Eds.), *Social work practice with Asian Americans* (pp. 125-142). Newbury Park, CA: Sage.

> The author provides a summary of major points in Confucian philosophy pertaining to human service, social welfare, and ideals of social harmony. This forms the basis for a model of social transformation relevant to practice with Asian Americans and to innovations in social work generally. The Gandhian approach to social action is compared with this.

Chung, D., & Haynes, A. W. (1993). Confucian welfare philosophy and social change technology: An integrated approach for international social development. *International Social Work, 36,* 37-46.

4. Christianity

Abbott, S. D., Garland, D. R., Huffman-Nevins, A., & Stewart, J. B. (1990). Social workers' views of local churches as service providers: Impressions from an exploratory study. *Social Work and Christianity, 17*(1), 7-16.

Ahn, Y. H. K. (1987). *The Korean Protestant church: The role in service delivery for Korean immigrants.* Unpublished doctoral dissertation, Columbia University.

Amato-von Hemert, K. (1995). *Towards a social work imagination: Reinhold Neibuhr on social work, sin, love and justice, a hermeneutic exploration.* Unpublished doctoral dissertation, University of Chicago.

Bachmann, E. T. (Ed.). (1955). *Churches and social welfare: Vol. 1. The activating concern.* New York: National Council of the Churches of Christ in the USA.

Bachmann, E. T. (Ed.). (1956). *Churches and social welfare: Vol. 3. The emerging concern.* New York: National Council of the Churches of Christ in the USA.

Ballenger, E. M. (1987). Racism: A crisis of spirituality. *Social Work and Christianity, 14*(2), 88-98.

Beaman-Hall, L., & Nason-Clark, N. (1997). Partners or protagonists? The transition house movement and conservative churches. *Affilia, 12*(2), 176-196.

Benton, J. F. (1981). A theology of charity for Christian social agencies. *Social Thought, 7*(4). 2-13.

Biestek, F. P. (1956). Religion and social casework. In L. C. DeSantis (Ed.), *The social welfare forum* (pp. 86-95). New York: Columbia University Press.

> **This is one of the earliest essays to criticize the frequent neglect of religion (particularly in its Judeo-Christian form) within social work. The author explains that religion provides important insights into human purpose and morality that can guide social casework.**

Bigham, T. J. (1956). Cooperation between ministers and social workers. In F. E. Johnson (Ed.), *Religion and social work* (pp. 141-154). New York: Institute for Religious and Social Studies, Harper and Brothers.

Breton, M. (1989). Liberation theology, group work, and the right of the poor and oppressed to participate in the life of the community. *Social Work with Groups, 12*(3), 5-18.

Canda, E. R. (1990). An holistic approach to prayer for social work practice. *Social Thought, 16*(3), 3-13.

Caplis, R. (1983). Catholic social service and transcendental values. *Social Thought, 9*(1), 3-16.

> **The author argues that Catholic Charities agencies should increase their incorporation of Christian spiritual beliefs and practices. On the basis of a review of Protestant, Catholic, and humanistic therapeutic literature, she advocates for further study and use of prayer, faith, and theological values.**

Cayton, H. R., & Nishi, S. M. (1955). *Churches and social welfare: Vol. 2. The changing scene.* New York: National Council of the Churches in Christ in the USA.

Conrad, A. P. (1980). Social ministry in early church: An integral component of the Christian community. *Social Thought, 6*(2), 41-51.

> Catholic theology and biblical and historical materials are reviewed to describe the integration of gospel proclamation, Christian community building, and social service in the early Christian church.

Consiglio, W. E. (1987). *Spirit-led helping: A model for evangelical social work counseling.* St. Davids, PA: North American Association of Christians in Social Work.

> The author provides a framework for clinical social workers who wish to practice from an explicit Christian evangelical perspective. Issues of Christian beliefs, values, and helping practices are integrated with social work.

Coughlin, B. J. (1965). A growing issue in church and state. *Social Work, 10,* 77-84.

Coughlin, B. J. (1965). *Church and state in social welfare.* New York: Columbia University Press.

Coughlin, B. J. (1970). Religious values and child welfare. *Social Casework, 51*(2), 82-90.

Davies, S. P. (1956). The churches and the non-sectarian agencies. In F. E. Johnson (Ed.), *Religion and social work* (pp. 81-95). New York: Institute for Religious and Social Studies, Harper and Brothers.

Denomme, M. J. (1987). *Religion and social policy during the Great Society era: An analysis of Protestant periodicals, 1964–1968.* Unpublished doctoral dissertation, Bryn Mawr College.

Denton, R. T. (1990). The religiously fundamentalist family: Training for assessment and treatment. *Journal of Social Work Education, 26,* 6-14.

> The author reviews conceptual and empirical research on fundamentalist (mainly Christian) family beliefs and lifestyles. While potential problems are identified, common negative stereotypes are questioned. Suggestions are given for including content on religion and fundamentalism into social work education.

DiBlasio, F. A. (1988). Integrative strategies for family therapy with Evangelical Christians. *Journal of Psychology and Theology, 16*(2), 127-134.

DiBlasio, F. A., & Benda, B. B. (1993). Practitioners, religion, and the use of forgiveness in the clinical setting. In E. Worthington, Jr. (Ed.), *Psychotherapy and religious values. Psychology and Christianity* (vol. 7, pp. 183-190). Grand Rapids, MI: Baker Book House.

> The authors discuss clinical practitioners' views and uses of religiously based practices that encourage therapeutic forgiveness. Indications for professionally appropriate use of forgiveness are suggested.

Doe, S. J. (1989). *Christian perspectives on poverty: An ideological foundation for social work, 1880-1920.* Unpublished doctoral dissertation, Washington University.

Evans, E. N. (1992). Liberation theology, empowerment theory and social work practice with the oppressed. *International Social Work, 35*(2), 135-147.

> **Ideas from Latin American–originated liberation theology (Christian) and secular empowerment theory are connected in this article. They provide a conceptual framework for understanding the social action processes of skill building, self-efficacy, and consciousness raising.**

Elliot, M. (1984). The church-related social worker. *Social Work and Christianity, 11*(2), 40-45.

Faver, C. A. (1989). Spirituality, faith, and social change: A case study of Vida Dutton Scudder. *Social Thought, 15*(1), 2-17.

Faver, C. A. (1991). Creative apostle of reconciliation: The spirituality and social philosophy of Emily Greene Balch. *Women's Studies, 18,* 335-351

Filinson, R. (1988). A model for church-based services for frail elderly persons and their families. *The Gerontologist, 28*(4), 483-486.

Fisher, A. L. (1978). Mormon welfare programs: Past and present. *Social Science Journal, 15*(2), 75-91.

Furman, L. D., Perry, D., & Goldade, T. (1996). Interaction of evangelical Christians and social workers in the rural environment. *Human Services in the Rural Environment, 19*(2/3), 5-8.

> **Results of a quantitative exploratory survey of rural evangelical Christians are presented with regard to their use of social workers. Results indicated that the participants tend to view social workers as less religious and more liberal than themselves, leading to reluctance to use their services.**

Garland, D. R. (1985). Volunteer ministry to families of prisoners and the Christian social worker's role. *Social Work and Christianity, 12*(1), 13-25.

Garland, D. R., & Bailey, P. L. (1990). Effective work with religious organizations by social workers in other settings. *Social Work and Christianity, 17*(2), 79-95.

Garland, D. S. R. (1984). The social worker and the pastoral counselor: Strangers or collaborators? *Social Work and Christianity, 10*(2), 22-41.

Garland, D. S. R. (1985). Family life education, family ministry, and church social work: Suggested relationships. *Social Work and Christianity, 12*(2), 14-26.

Garland, D. S. R. (Ed.). (1992). *Church social work: Helping the whole person in the context of the church.* St. Davids, PA: North American Association of Christians in Social Work.

> **This collection gives an overview of Christian church, community-based social services. It addresses history, ideology, programs, direct practice, administrative and organizational structures, and international issues.**

Garland, D. S. R., & Bailey, P. L. (1990). Effective work with religious organizations by social workers in other settings. *Social Work and Christianity, 17*(2), 79-95.

Gatza, M. (1979). The role of healing prayer in the helping professions. *Social Thought, 5*(2), 3-13.

Genz, W. J. (1982). *The making of a progressive.* Unpublished doctoral dissertation, Bryn Mawr College.

Gerdes, D. E., Beck, M. N., Cowan-Hancock, S., & Wilkinson-Sparks, T. (1996). Adult survivors of childhood sexual abuse: The case of Mormon women. *Affilia, 11*(1), 39-60.

Gill, V. E. (1984). Homosexuality: A reparative view. *Social Work and Christianity, 11*(2), 10-28.

Glenn, M. W. (1922). Social casework and spiritual values. *The Family, 3*(4), 121-124.

Gluchman, V. (1991). The social activities of the Slovak Lutheran church. *Spirituality and Social Work Communicator, 2*(1), 3-5.

Gluchman, V. (1997). *Slovak Lutheran social ethics.* Lewiston, England: Edwin Mellon.

> **The author provides a historical and philosophical analysis of the development of social ethics within Slovak Lutheranism. Positive and negative consequences on Slovak society and social service are examined. This is a rare presentation in English of central European social service ideology in relation to religion and politics.**

Gottfried, G. M. (1992). *Qualitative analysis of child-caring experiences of religious sisters.* Unpublished doctoral dissertation, Case Western Reserve University.

Haber, D. (1984). Church-based mutual help groups for caregivers of noninstitutionalized elders. *Journal of Religion and Aging, 1*(1), 63-69.

Hall, S. (1979). The common chest concept: Luther's contribution to 16th century poor relief reform. *Social Thought, 5*(1), 43-53.

Hess, J. J., Jr. (1980). Social work's identity crisis: A Christian anthropological response. *Social Thought, 6*(1), 59-69.

Hildebrandt, R. R. (1978). *The history of a developing social responsibility among Lutherans through cooperation efforts of the church bodies and the place of social welfare in the mission of the Lutheran church today.* Unpublished doctoral dissertation, Tulane University.

Himes, K. R. (1986). The local church as a mediating structure. *Social Thought, 12*(1), 23-30.

Holman, R. (1984). The Christian social worker: A British view. *Social Work and Christianity, 11*, 48-60.

Horsburgh, M. (1987). Christianity and social work: Some practice issues. *Social Work and Christianity, 54*(2), 63-77.

Horsburgh, M. (1988). Words and deeds: Christianity and social welfare. *Australian Social Work, 41*(2), 17-23.

Horton, A. L., & Williamson, J. A. (Eds.). (1988). *Abuse and religion: When praying isn't enough.* Lexington, MA: Lexington Books.

Hubbard, H. (1980). A call to harvest, ministry to America. *Social Thought, 6*(1), 27-39.

Humphrey, R. A. (1980). Religion in Appalachia: Implications for social work practice. *Journal of Humanics, 8*(2), 4-18.

Iannaccone, L. R., & Miles, C. A. (1990). Dealing with social change: The Mormon church's response to change in women's roles. *Social Forces, 68*(4), 1231-1250.

Ireland, E. C. (1991). *The role of the Pentecostal church as a service provider in the Puerto Rican community, Boston, MA: A case study*. Unpublished doctoral dissertation, Brandeis University.

Johnson, T. J. (1990). Empowerment as a Christian helping strategy: Bridging the chasm between client and institutional oppression. *Social Work and Christianity, 17*(2), 66-78.

Johnstone, B. V. (1986). The theory and strategy of the seamless garment. *Social Thought, 12*(4), 19-27.

Joseph, M. V. (1975). The parish as a social service and social action center: An ecological systems approach. *Social Thought, 1*(2), 43-59.

Joseph, M. V., & Conrad, A. P. (1980). A parish neighborhood model for social work practice. *Social Casework, 61*(7), 423-432.

> **Catholic parish-based services for the neighborhood community are described as natural helping networks. This forms the basis of a model for community-based social work practice.**

Judah, E. H. (1985). A spirituality of professional service: A sacramental model. *Social Thought, 11*(4), 25-35.

Keith-Lucas, A. (1960). Some notes on theology and social work. *Social Casework, 41*(2), 87-91.

Keith-Lucas, A. (1985). Interpreting Christian social work principles to the secular world. *Social Work and Christianity, 12*(2), 40-43.

Keith-Lucas, A. (1985). *So you want to be a social worker: A primer for the Christian student*. St. Davids, PA: North American Association of Christians in Social Work.

> **The author presents a framework of values and practice suggestions for social work students who wish to practice from an explicit Christian orientation. Advice is given about how to be faithful to Christian commitments and to social work values of client self-determination and nonjudgmental acceptance of clients.**

Keith-Lucas, A. (1988). Does social work need Christians? *Social Work and Christianity, 15*(1), 16-22.

Keith-Lucas, A. (1994). *Giving and taking help* (rev. ed.). St. Davids, PA: North American Association of Christians in Social Work.

Kelly, J. R. (1986). Residual or prophetic? The cultural fate of Roman Catholic sexual ethics of abortion and contraception. *Social Thought, 12*(2), 3-18.

Kim, M. (1989). *Korean-American clergymen's views on mental health and treatment.* Unpublished doctoral dissertation, University of California at Berkeley.

King, N. (1965). Some perspectives on theology and social work. In P. C. McCabe & F. J. Turner (Eds.), *Catholic social work: A contemporary overview* (pp. 6-27). Ottawa: Catholic Charities Council of Canada.

Kreutziger, S. S. (1995). Spirituality in faith. *Reflections: Narratives of Professional Helping, 1*(4), 28-35.

Kuhlmann, E. G. (1982). *A Christian interpretation of humanity for social work.* Unpublished doctoral dissertation, Messiah College.

Kwon-Ahn, Y. H. (1987). *The Korean Protestant church: The role in service delivery for Korean immigrants.* Unpublished doctoral dissertation, Columbia University.

Lee, D. B. (1991). Bridging the gap between clergy and laity. *Spirituality and Social Work Communicator, 2*(1), 5-7.

Lehmacher, E. K. (1997). The parish or church social worker's counseling role. *Social Work and Christianity, 24*(1), 34-57.

Leiby, J. (1984). Charity organization reconsidered. *Social Service Review, 58,* 523-538.

Manthey, B. (1989). *Social work, religion and the church: Policy implications.* Unpublished doctoral dissertation, University of Texas at Austin.

Mayo, L. W. (1956). Spiritual factors in social work. In F. E. Johnson (Ed.), *Religion and social work* (pp. 71-79). New York: Institute for Religious and Social Studies, Harper and Brothers.

McCabe, P. C. (1965). Sectarian social work—necessity or luxury. In P. C. McCabe & F. J. Turner (Eds.), *Catholic social work: A contemporary overview* (pp. 28-43). Ottawa: Catholic Charities Council of Canada.

McKinney, E. A. (1980). A school of social work trains urban indigenous leadership in Cleveland. *Community Development Journal, 15*(3), 200-207.

Midgley, J. (1990). The new Christian right, social policy, and the welfare state. *Journal of Sociology and Social Welfare, 17*(2), 89-106.

> **This article summarizes and critiques biblical texts and political discourse used by conservative evangelical Protestants in the "New Christian Right" to oppose state welfare. The author provides this knowledge to stimulate and widen debate and analysis of rival views of social policy.**

National Conference of Catholic Charities. (1983). *A code of ethics.* Washington, DC: Author.

Netting, F. E. (1982). Secular and religious funding in church-related agencies. *Social Service Review, 56,* 586-604.

Netting, F. E. (1982). Social work and religious values in church-related agencies. *Social Work and Christianity, 9*(1-2), 4-20.

Netting, F. E. (1984). Church-related agencies and social welfare. *Social Service Review, 58,* 404-420.

> Findings from an exploratory study of three groups of Protestant, religiously affiliated agencies are presented. The author analyzes variations in their perception of church affiliation and its impact on service. Implications for research and policy are given.

Niebuhr, R. (1932). *The contribution of religion to social work.* New York: Columbia University Press.

> A prominent theologian analyzes the history and contributions of religion (primarily Christianity) to the development of social work. The author critiques authoritarian and oppressive features of institutional religion while emphasizing positive values of Christian social ethics. This illustrates controversies in sectarian social work early in the profession's history.

Ortiz, L. P., & Kuhlmann, E. G. (1988). NACSW looks at itself: Some survey results. *Social Work and Christianity, 15*(1), 23-32.

Ortiz, L. P. A. (1990). Ideology: The hidden force in social work practice. *Social Work and Christianity, 17*(2), 96-108.

Pepper, A. R. (1956). Protestant social work today. In F. E. Johnson (Ed.), *Religion and social work* (pp. 17-27). New York: Institute for Religious and Social Studies, Harper and Brothers.

Peterman, P. J. (1990). *Help seeking patterns of black women in selected black churches.* Unpublished doctoral dissertation, Columbia University.

Reid, W. J., & Simpson, P. K. (1987). Sectarian agencies. In A. Minahan (Ed.), *Encyclopedia of social work* (pp. 545-556). Silver Spring, MD: National Association of Social Workers.

Ressler, L. E. (1992). Theologically enriched social work: Alan Keith-Lucas' approach to social work and religion. *Spirituality and Social Work Journal, 3*(2), 14-20.

Ressler, L. E. (Ed.). (1994). *Hearts strangely warmed: Reflections on biblical passages relevant to social work.* St. Davids, PA: North American Association of Christians in Social Work.

Ryan, J. A. (1983). A practical philosophy of social work. *Social Thought, 9*(4), 4-9.

Scharper, P. J. (1975). The theology of liberation: Some reflections. *Social Thought, 1*(1), 59-66.

Scudder, H. S. (1990). Social work and pastoral counseling perspectives: An exploratory comparative analysis. *Social Work and Christianity, 17*(1), 37-51.

Servetto, E. (1985). Addressing the needs of depressed Christian clients: A review of selected behavioral science and Christian perspectives. *Social Work and Christianity, 12*(2), 27-39.

Sherwood, D. A. (1997). Freedom, responsibility, and the common good: A Christian view of social justice in a pluralistic world. *Social Work and Christianity, 24*(1), 19-33.

Smith, K. G. (1984). Developing a Christian counseling ministry in the local church: A proven model. *Social Work and Christianity, 11*(2), 29-39.

Smith, R. (1961). Spiritual, ethical and moral values for children in foster care. *Child Welfare, 40*(1), 20-24.

Sneck, W. J., & Bonica, R. P. (1980). Attempting the integration of psychology and spirituality. *Social Thought, 6*(3), 27-36.

Spressart, J. (1992). Social action and the church. In D. S. R. Garland (Ed.), *Church social work: Helping the whole person in the context of the church* (pp. 102-119). St. Davids, PA: North American Association of Christians in Social Work.

Swift, A. L., Jr. (1956). The church and human welfare. In F. E. Johnson (Ed.), *Religion and social work* (pp. 1-15). New York: Institute for Religious and Social Studies. Harper and Brothers.

Tillich, P. (1962). The philosophy of social work. *Social Service Review, 36*, 13-16.

Tropman, J. E. (1986). The "Catholic ethic" vs. the "Protestant ethic": Catholic social service and the welfare state. *Social Thought, 12*(1), 13-22.

Turner, F. J. (1983). Competence: A key to healing in a broken world. *Social Work and Christianity, 10*(2), 42-53.

Van Hook, M. P. (1997). Christian social work. In R. L. Edwards (Ed.-in-Chief), *Encyclopedia of social work* (19th ed., Suppl., pp. 68-77). Washington, DC: NASW Press.

> **The author provides a succinct summary of the history, belief system, scriptural foundation, and institutional forms of social work occurring within both Catholic and Protestant denominations in the United States.**

Vitillo, R. J. (1986). Parish-based social ministry: From a theological and historical perspective. *Social Thought, 12*(3), 30-38.

Voss, R. W. (1985). A sociological analysis and theological reflection on adoption services in Catholic Charities agencies. *Social Thought, 11*(1), 32-43.

Whipple, E. B. (1984). A study of maturational patterns among new converts. *Social Work and Christianity, 11*(1), 31-47.

York, G. Y. (1989). Strategies for managing the religious-based denial of rural clients. *Human Services in the Rural Environment, 13*(2), 16-22.

5. Existentialism and Humanism

Bradford, K. A. (1969). *Existentialism and casework*. New York: Exposition Press.

Brown, J. A. (1980). Child abuse: An existential process. *Clinical Social Work Journal, 8*(2), 108-115.

Brown, J. A., & Romanchuk, B. J. (1994). Existential social work practice with the aged: Theory and practice. *Journal of Gerontological Social Work, 23*(1/2), 49-65.

Charny, I. W. (1986). An existential/dialectical model for analyzing marital functioning and interaction. *Family Process, 25*(4), 571-589.

Dean, R. G., & Fenby, B. L. (1989). Exploring epistemologies: Social work action as a reflection of philosophical assumptions. *Journal of Social Work Education, 25*, 46-54.

Edwards, D. G. (1982). *Existential psychotherapy: The process of caring*. New York: Gardner.

> **A clinical social worker provides an exposition of core existentialist concepts and helping approaches in relation to psychotherapy. Special attention is given to the development of self, choice, and sharing of worlds in the helping relationship.**

Falck, H. S. (1978). Crisis theory and social group work. *Social Work with Groups, 1*(1), 75-84.

Gottesfeld, M. L. (1984). The self-psychology of Heinz Kohut: An existential reading. *Clinical Social Work Journal, 12*(4), 283-291.

Guttman, D. (1996). *Logotherapy for the helping professional: Meaningful social work*. New York: Springer.

> **This book explains the psychotherapeutic perspective and techniques of Victor Frankl, the founder of logotherapy. The practice approach assists clinical social workers to apply logotherapy in practice and to reduce their own stress and burnout.**

Imre, R. W. (1971). A theological view of social casework. *Social Casework, 52*(9), 578-585.

> **The author presents key existentialist ideas and values for a humane approach to casework, mainly from Christian and Jewish theologians.**

King, M. E., & Citrenbaum, C. M. (1993). *Existential hypnotherapy*. New York: Guilford.

Klugman, D. (1997). Existentialism and constructivism: A bi-polar model of subjectivity. *Clinical Social Work Journal, 25*(3), 297-313.

Krill, D. F. (1966). Existentialism: A philosophy for our current revolutions. *Social Service Review, 40*, 289-301.

Krill, D. F. (1969). Existential psychotherapy and the problem of anomie. *Social Work, 14*(2), 33-49.

Krill, D. F. (1978). *Existential social work*. New York: Free Press.

> **This book is a thorough and systematic presentation of existentialist approaches to theory, values, and helping activities specifically related to social work practice.**

Krill, D. F. (1986). *The beat worker: Humanizing social work and psychotherapy*. Lanham, MD: University Press of America.

Krill, D. F. (1988). Existential social work. In R. A. Dorfman (Ed.), *Paradigms of clinical social work* (pp. 295-316). New York: Brunner/Mazel.

Krill, D. F. (1990). *Practice wisdom: A guide for the helping professional*. Newbury Park, CA: Sage.

> **The author presents self-exploration learning exercises, with explanations rooted in existentialism, that can be used in classroom or individual education.**

They emphasize development of skills in self-understanding, creativity, intuition, and spontaneity.

Krill, D. F. (1995). My spiritual sojourn into existential social work. *Reflections: Narratives of Professional Helping, 1*(4), 57-64.

Krill, D. F. (1996). Existential social work. In F. J. Turner (Ed.), *Social work treatment: Interlocking theoretical approaches* (4th ed., pp. 250-281). New York: Free Press.

Lantz, J. (1987). The use of Frankl's concepts in family therapy. *Journal of Independent Social Work, 2*(2), 65-80.

Lantz, J. (1993). *Existential family therapy: Using the concepts of Victor Frankl.* Northvale, NJ: Aronson.

Therapeutic interventions and concepts developed by Victor Frankl, the founder of logotherapy, are presented in a collection of articles on family therapy and family services for diverse populations and practice situations.

Lantz, J. (1994). Marcel's "availability" in existential psychotherapy with couples and families. *Contemporary Family Therapy, 16*(6), 489-501.

Lantz, J. (1996). The existential psychotherapist as a host in couples therapy. In B. J. Brothers (Ed.), *Couples: Building bridges* (pp. 67-78). Binghamton, NY: Haworth.

Lantz, J., & Alford, K. (1995). Art in existential psychotherapy with couples and families. *Contemporary Family Therapy, 17*(3), 331-342.

Lantz, J., & Alford, K. (1995). Existential family treatment with an urban Appalachian adolescent. *Journal of Family Psychotherapy, 6*(4), 15-27.

Lantz, J., & Greenlee, R. (1990). Existential social work with Vietnam veterans. *Journal of Independent Social Work, 5*(1), 39-52.

Lantz, J., & Kondrat, M. E. (1997). Evaluation research problems in existential psychotherapy with couples and families. *Journal of Family Psychotherapy, 8*(2), 55-72.

Lantz, J., & Pegram, M. (1989). Casework and restoration of meaning. *Social Casework, 70*(9), 549-555.

Sim, S. (1994). The answer lies in the verb 'to be': An existentialist feminist perspective on the casework relationship. *Australian Social Work, 47*(2), 25-32.

Sinsheimer, R. B. (1969). The existential casework relationship. *Social Casework, 50*(2), 67-73.

Solomon, E. L. (1967). Humanistic values and social casework. *Social Casework, 48*(1), 26-32.

Stretch, J. J. (1967). Existentialism: A proposed philosophical orientation for social work. *Social Work, 12*(4), 97-102.

Weiss, D. (1975). *Existential human relations.* Montreal: Dawson College Press.

6. Gandhian Social Activism

Capozzi, L. (1992). Nonviolent social work and stress reduction: A Gandhian cognitive restructuring model. *Spirituality and Social Work Journal, 3*(1), 13-18.

Dasgupta, S. (1986). Gandhi and the new society. *Social Development Issues, 10*(1), 1-10.

Pandey, R. S. (1996). Gandhian perspectives on personal empowerment and social development. *Social Development Issues, 18*(2), 66-84.

> **Mahatma Gandhi's paradigm of nonviolent social action is presented with a glossary of related Indian terms. Nonviolent change is described as a dialectical and proactive process of personal development and social change that moves toward realization of truth and justice for all sectors of society.**

Sharma, S. (1987). Development, peace, and nonviolent social change: The Gandhian perspective. *Social Development Issues, 10*(3), 31-45.

Walz, T., Sharma, S., & Birnbaum, C. (1990). *Gandhian thought as theory base for social work.* (University of Illinois School of Social Work Occasional Paper Series I.) Urbana-Champaign, IL: University of Illinois School of Social Work.

> **This monograph gives an introduction to Gandhi's principles of nonviolent social change and explains their implications for professional social work.**

7. Hinduism (see also A.6 & B.2)

Bhattacharya, V. (1965). Swami Vivekananda's message of service. *Social Welfare, 12*(1), 1-3.

Karnik, S. J., Suri, B. (1995). The law of karma and social work considerations. *International Social Work, 38*(4), 365-77.

> **The author explains the law of karma as a predominant belief in India. Its relation to social dynamics concerning caste and other social issues is described. A case study and a social work practice approach for addressing these issues are presented.**

Patel, I. (1987). *Vivekananda's approach to social work.* Mylapore, India: Sri Ramakvishna Math.

> **Swami Vivekananda's philosophy of social work, called karma yoga (spiritual discipline of action for service), is presented in detail. Related human service programs in India are described. The author discusses social work in volunteer and professional modes as a practice that can lead to spiritual realization. This is an unusually thorough English language presentation of an Asian spiritual approach to social work.**

Saini, S. (1989). *Cultural identification and perceived sources of influences in decision-making among Hindu adolescents.* Unpublished doctoral dissertation, Adelphi University.

Valenzuela, W. G. (1978). *Meeting human needs: The Ananda Ashrama: An indigenous therapeutic milieu.* Unpublished doctoral dissertation, University of California at Berkeley.

Vivekananda, S. (1984). *Karma yoga.* Calcutta, India: Advaita Ashrama.

8. Islam

Al-Krenawi, A. (1996). Group work with Bedouin widows of the Negev in a medical clinic. *Affilia, 11*(3), 303-318.

> The author describes the Islamic cultural and religious context of Bedouin widows. Clinical group work designed to help these women to deal with loss and grief issues is discussed.

Al-Krenawi, A., & Graham, J. R. (1996). Social work and traditional healing rituals among the Bedouin of the Negev, Israel. *International Social Work, 39*(2), 177-188.

Al-Krenawi, A., & Graham, J. R. (1997). Spirit possession and exorcism in the treatment of a Bedouin psychiatric patient. *Clinical Social Work Journal, 25*(2), 211-222.

Ali, A. (1990). An approach to the Islamization of social and behavioral sciences. *American Journal of Islamic Social Sciences, 6*(2), 37-58.

Haynes, A. W., Eweiss, M. M. I., Mageed, L. M. A., & Chung, D. K. (1997). Islamic social transformation: Considerations for the social worker. *International Social Work, 40*(3), 264-275.

> The historical and scriptural (Qur'anic) basis of Sunni Islamic social welfare ideology is presented. Based on their "Islamic social transformation model," the authors advocate for innovations in social work practice with Islamic populations and in the profession generally.

Jain, N. (1965). Zakat: A Muslim way of helping the needy. *Social Welfare, 12*(1), 4-5.

Wain, M. A. (1996). Enforcement of mahr by Muslim women: A case of reconsideration. *Indian Journal of Social Work, 57*(2), 295-307.

9. Judaism

Abramowitz, L. (1993). Prayer as therapy among the frail Jewish elderly. *Journal of Gerontological Social Work, 19*(3/4), 69-75.

Ansel, E. (1973). T'shuva—parallels to the existential growth process. *Jewish Social Work Forum, 10*(2), 36-47.

Berl, F. (1979). Clinical practice in a Jewish context. *Journal of Jewish Communal Service, 55*(4), 366-368.

Berman, S. (1976). Value perspectives on Jewish family life. *Social Casework, 57*(6), 366-372.

Blum, D. C., Lefkowitz, S., & Levy, N. (1976). Jewish consciousness and social work values at Wurzweiler: A research study. *Jewish Social Work Forum, 12*, 67-78.

Bubis, G. B. (1980). The Jewish component in Jewish communal service—from theory to practice. *Journal of Jewish Communal Service, 56*(3), 227-237.

> **The author presents a summary of historical, cultural, and geopolitical factors affecting Jewish identity. He advocates a set of principles for culturally and religiously grounded Jewish communal service along with related controversies in the Jewish community and social work profession.**

Bubis, G. B. (1981). Professional trends in Jewish communal practice in America. *Journal of Jewish Communal Service, 57*(4), 304-311.

Bubis, G. B. (1986). The aging Jewish community: The dynamics of choice. *Journal of Jewish Communal Service, 62*(4), 292-298.

Bunim, S. S. (1987). *Religious and secular factors of role strain in Orthodox Jewish mothers.* Unpublished doctoral dissertation, Yeshiva University.

Eilberg, A. (1984). Views of human development in Jewish rituals: A comparison with Eriksonian theory. *Smith College Studies in Social Work, 55*(1), 1-23.

Eskenazi, D. (1983). God concepts and community structure. *Journal of Jewish Communal Service, 59*(3), 217-227.

Feinberg, S. S., & Feinberg, K. G. (1985). An assessment of mental health needs of the Orthodox Jewish population of metropolitan New York. *Journal of Jewish Communal Service, 62*(1), 29-39.

Gelman, S. R., & Schnall, D. J. (1997). Jewish communal service. In R. L. Edwards (Ed.-in-Chief), *Encyclopedia of social work* (19th ed., Suppl., pp. 169-178). Washington, DC: NASW Press.

> **The authors present an introduction to the history and ideology of Jewish communal service. Contemporary patterns of institutional organization and practice regarding family and community service for the Jewish community are described.**

Gold, I. H. (1970). Sectarian services in a time of crisis. *Jewish Social Work Forum, 7*(1), 5-13.

Kahn, N. E. (1995). The adult bat mitzvah: Its use in the articulation of women's identity. *Affilia, 10*(3), 299-314.

> **The ceremony of bat mitzvah for Jewish women is discussed. The author explains how it can contribute to a clarification of Jewish identity and affirmation of women's experience and roles.**

Kahn, W. (1985). Jewish communal service and the professional—today and tomorrow. *Journal of Jewish Communal Service, 62*(2), 111-117.

Karp, B. I. (1987). A specialist in Jewish education within a family and children's agency. *Journal of Jewish Communal Service, 64*(1), 69-76.

Levin, M. (1970). Sectarian services in a time of crisis. *Jewish Social Work Forum, 7*(1), 14-27.

Levine, E. (1990). The ethical ritual in Judaism: A review of sources on Torah study and social action. *Jewish Social Work Forum, 26,* 44-50.

> **The author advocates that Jewish social workers should be familiar with ethical teachings of Torah and Jewish tradition so that they can be adapted to more effective practice in contemporary society.**

Levine, E. M. (1994). *Communities in conflict: Social and religious movements in Jewish life.* Unpublished doctoral dissertation, Yeshiva University.

Linzer, N. (1978). Synagogue, classroom, and communal atmosphere for a wholesome Jewish family development. *Jewish Social Work Forum, 14,* 55-70.

Linzer, N. (1979). A Jewish philosophy of social work practice. *Journal of Jewish Communal Service, 55*(4), 309-317.

Mason, S. J. (1978). Jews in social work. *Journal of Reform Judaism, 25*(3), 79-83.

Miller, C. (1980). Commitment, ideology, and skill. *Journal of Jewish Communal Service, 57*(1), 30-36.

Nulman, E. (1982). Is the Jewish community (truly) treating the Jewish family? *Journal of Jewish Communal Service, 59*(1), 66-72.

Nussbaum, D. (1983). Tsedakah, social justice, and human rights. *Journal of Jewish Communal Service, 59*(3), 228-236.

> **The traditional Jewish principle of tsedakah (communal welfare) is analyzed for the ways it has both supported and inhibited social justice and egalitarianism. The author proposes a revaluation of the principle to make it more conducive to social justice in the contemporary global social context.**

Ostrov, S. (1976). A family therapist's approach to working with an Orthodox Jewish clientele. *Journal of Jewish Communal Service, 63*(2), 147-154.

Schector, M. (1971). A value system model in Jewish social welfare. *Jewish Social Work Forum, 8*(2), 5-22.

Schindler, R. (1987). Intergenerational theories in social work intervention with religious Jewish families. *Journal of Social Work and Policy in Israel, 1,* 99-113.

Spero, M. H. (1981). A clinical note on the therapeutic management of "religious" resistances in Orthodox Jewish clientele. *Journal of Jewish Communal Service, 57*(4). 334-341.

Spero, M. H. (1986). *Handbook of psychotherapy and Jewish ethics: Halakhic perspectives on professional values and techniques.* Jerusalem: Feldheim.

Spero, M. H. (1987). Identity and individuality in the nouveau-religious patient: Theoretical and clinical aspects. *Journal of Social Work and Policy in Israel, 1,* 25-49.

Sprafkin, B. R. (1970). Sectarian services in a time of crisis. *Jewish Social Work Forum, 7*(1), 36-45.

Wikler, M. (1977). The Torah view of mental illness: Sin or sickness? *Journal of Jewish Communal Service, 53*(4), 338-344.

Wikler, M. (1986). Pathways to treatment: How Orthodox Jews enter therapy. *Social Casework, 67*(2), 113-118.

> The author describes values and community patterns in the Orthodox Jewish community that affect the provision of mental health services. Some barriers to cooperation are identified along with suggestions to enhance trust and referral to mental health professionals by leaders in the Orthodox community.

10. Shamanism and Neo-Shamanism (see also A.11, B.3, & B.4)

Canda, E. R. (1983). General implications of shamanism for clinical social work. *International Social Work, 26*(4), 14-22.

> This article describes features of shamanism that are common across many cultures. The author advocates respect for shamanistic traditions and community-based healers, and gives suggestions for ways that clinical social workers can learn from shamanism to enhance spiritually sensitive and ecologically concerned practice.

Cataldo, C. (1979). Wilderness therapy: Modern day shamanism. In C. B. Germain (Ed.), *Social work practice: People and environments* (pp. 46-73). New York: Columbia University Press.

Frey, L. A., & Edinburg, G. (1978). Helping, manipulation, and magic. *Social Work, 23*, 89-93.

Laird, J. (1984). Sorcerers, shamans, and social workers: The use of ritual in social work practice. *Social Work, 29*, 123-128.

> Insights from anthropology, family therapy, and social work are combined to give guidelines for the assessment of clients' use of rituals in daily life. Based on analogies from shamanism and other healing traditions, the author provides suggestions about how to help clients use rituals in ways that are creative and affirming.

11. Spiritism, Santeria, and Curanderismo (see also A.10 & B.3)

Berthold, S. M. (1989). Spiritism as a form of psychotherapy: Implications for social work practice. *Social Casework, 70*(8), 502-509.

De la Rosa, M. (1988). Puerto Rican spiritualism: A key dimension for effective social casework practice with Puerto Ricans. *International Social Work, 31*(4), 273-283.

Delgado, M. (1977). Puerto Rican spiritism and the social work profession. *Social Casework, 58*(8), 451-458.

Delgado, M. (1988). Groups in Puerto Rican spiritism: Implications for clinicians. In C. Jacobs & D. D. Bowles (Eds.), *Ethnicity and race: Critical concepts in social work* (pp. 34-47). Silver Spring, MD: National Association of Social Workers.

> Dynamics of leadership and healing processes in Puerto Rican spiritist rituals are analyzed in terms of group work methods and psychodrama.

Krajewski-Jaime, E. R. (1991). Folk-healing among Mexican-American families as a consideration in the delivery of child welfare and child health care services. *Child Welfare, 60*(2), 157-167.

Krassner, M. (1986). Effective features of therapy from the healer's perspective: A study of Curanderismo. *Smith College Studies in Social Work, 56*(3), 157-183.

Paulino, A. (1995). Spiritism, santeria, brujeria and voodooism: A comparative view of indigenous healing systems. *Journal of Teaching in Social Work, 12*(1/2), 105-124.

> **The author gives brief descriptions of several traditional healing systems commonly used by Caribbean immigrants at times of stress. The article advocates for specialized content on these practices in social work education.**

Sanville, J. (1975). Therapists in competition and cooperation with exorcists: The spirit world clinically revisited. *Clinical Social Work Journal, 3*(4), 286-297.

12. Taoism (see also B.2)

Caputo, R. K. (1988). The tao of evaluation: Deriving good from flawed methodology. *Administration in Social Work, 12*(3), 61-70.

Jordan, J. R. (1985). Paradox and polarity: The tao of family therapy. *Family Process, 24*(2), 165-174.

> **Insights from Taoist philosophy concerning harmony between opposites and the nature of change are applied to understanding family therapy and paradoxical intention techniques.**

Koenig, T. L., & Spano, R. N. (1998). Taoism and the strengths perspective. In E. R. Canda (Ed.), *Spirituality in social work: New directions* (pp. 47-65). Binghamton, NY: Haworth Pastoral Press.

> **The authors critique the contributions and limitations of the strengths perspective on social work practice based on central philosophical concepts of Taoism. They advocate for a holistic perspective beyond dichotomistic thinking. A case example illustrates the approach.**

13. Transpersonalism

Borenzweig, H. (1980). Jungian theory and social work practice. *Journal of Sociology and Social Welfare, 7*(4), 571-585.

Borenzweig, H. (1984). *Jung and social work.* New York: University Press of America.

> **This book is a detailed application of Jungian theory and techniques to social work practice. The author critiques the neglect of Jungian insights in social work, points out areas of compatibility, and suggests many ways that social work can enhance practice with individuals and groups.**

Canda, E. R. (1991). East/West philosophical synthesis in transpersonal theory. *Journal of Sociology and Social Welfare, 18*(4), 137-152.

Cowley, A. (1993). Transpersonal social work: A theory for the 1990s. *Social Work, 38,* 527-534.

Cowley, A. (1996). Transpersonal social work. In F. J. Turner (Ed.), *Social work treatment: Interlocking theoretical approaches* (4th ed., pp. 663-698). New York: Free Press.

> This chapter presents a summary of the history and major ideas of transpersonal psychological theories as applied to social work, especially as influenced by Ken Wilber. These theories focus on developmental processes and experiences that carry a person beyond a sense of identity limited by body and ego.

Grubbs, G. A. (1994). An abused child's use of sand play in the healing process. *Clinical Social Work Journal, 22*(2), 193-209.

McDonald, B. J. (1989). *A feminist critique of Ken Wilber's transpersonal psychological theory of human development.* Unpublished master's thesis, University of Iowa.

McGee, E. (1984). The transpersonal perspective: Implications for the future of personal and social development. *Social Development Issues, 8*(3), 151-181.

Smith, E. D. (1990). *The relationship of transpersonal development to the psychosocial distress of cancer patients.* Unpublished doctoral dissertation, Catholic University of America.

Snyder, F. R. (1988). *A study of Jungian personality typology and values of future administrators and social work clinicians.* Unpublished doctoral dissertation, Ohio State University.

Woodruff, L. K. (1996). Impediments to cooperation toward international social development: A Jungian perspective. *Social Work, 41,* 383-389.

B. Cultural Perspectives and Issues

1. African American

Allen-Meares, P. (1989). Adolescent sexuality and premature parenthood: Role of the Black church in prevention. *Journal of Social Work and Human Sexuality, 8*(1), 133-142.

Bolling, J. L. (1990). *The heart of soul: An Africentric approach to psychospiritual wholeness.* New York: Mandala Rising.

Brashears, F., & Roberts, M. (1996). The Black church as a resource for change. In S. L. Logan (Ed.), *The Black family: Strengths, self-help, and positive change* (pp. 181-192). Boulder, CO: Westview.

Burton, C. A., & Richardson, R. C. (1996). Following in faith: The study of an African-American caregiver. *Social Work and Christianity, 23*(2), 141-145.

Devore, W. (1983). Ethnic reality: The life model and work with black families. *Social Casework, 64*(9), 525-531.

Ford, M. E., Edwards, G., Rodriguez, J. L., Gibson, R. C., & Tilley, B. C. (1996). An empowerment centered, church-based asthma education program for African American adults. *Health and Social Work, 21*(1), 70-75.

Haber, D. (1984). Church-based programs for Black care givers for non-institutionalized elders. *Journal of Gerontologial Social Work, 7*(4), 43-55.

Karenga, M. (1995). Making the past meaningful: Kwanzaa and the concept of Sankofa. *Reflections: Narratives of Professional Helping, 1*(4), 36-46.

> **The founder of Kwanzaa, a nonsectarian celebration of African and African-American heritage and spirituality, describes its principles and origins.**

Logan, S. L. (1980). *The Black Baptist church: A social psychological study in coping and growth.* Unpublished doctoral dissertation, Columbia University.

Logan, S. L. (Ed.). (1996). *The Black family: Strengths, self-help, and positive change.* Boulder, CO: Westview.

> **This collection addresses various aspects of African-American spirituality in the context of history, culture, family life, resilience in response to oppression, and contemporary patterns of religious community support systems.**

Logan, S. L., Freeman, E. M., & McRoy, R. G. (1990). *Social work practice with Black families: A culturally specific perspective.* New York: Longman.

Morrison, J. D. (1991). The Black church as a support system for Black elderly. *Journal of Gerontological Social Work, 17*(1/2), 105-120.

O'Brien, P. (1995). From surviving to thriving: The complex experience of living in public housing. *Affilia, 10*(2), 155-78.

Peterman, P. J. (1990). *Help seeking patterns of black women in selected black churches.* Unpublished doctoral dissertation, Columbia University.

Schiele, J. H. (1994). Afrocentricity as an alternative world view for equality. *Journal of Progressive Human Services, 5*(1), 5-25.

Smith, J. M. (1993). Function and supportive roles of church and religion. In J. S. Jackson, L. M. Chatters, & R. J. Taylor (Eds.), *Aging in Black America* (pp. 124-147). Newbury Park, CA: Sage.

Taylor, R. J., & Chatters, L. M. (1986). Patterns of informal support to elderly black adults: Family, friends, and church members. *Social Work, 31,* 432-438.

Taylor, R. J., & Chatters, L. M. (1991). Religious life. In J. S. Jackson (Ed.), *Life in Black America* (pp. 105-123). Newbury Park, CA: Sage.

White, B. W., & Hampton, D. M. (1995). African American pioneers in social work. In R. L. Edwards (Ed.-in-Chief), *Encyclopedia of social work* (19th ed., pp. 101-115). Washington, DC: NASW Press.

> **The authors describe contributions of African Americans to the formation and early history of social work and social service. Some religious and spiritual themes and affiliations of these social work pioneers are mentioned.**

2. Asian and Asian American (see also A.2, A.3, A.6, A.7, & A.12)

Banerjee, G. R. (n. d.). *Papers on social work: An Indian perspective.* Bombay, India: Tata Institute of Social Science.

Banerjee, M. M. (1997). Frozen feta cheese lasagna with crushed hot peppers. *Reflections: Narratives of Professional Helping, 3*(4), 44-54.

Banerjee, M. M. (1997). Strengths despite constraints: Memoirs of research in a slum in Calcutta. *Reflections: Narratives of Professional Helping, 3*(3), 36-45.

> The author describes personal experiences and insights gained during a qualitative field study of the resilience of Hindu and Islamic residents of a slum in Calcutta.

Canda, E. R. (1991). *Philosophy of equilibrium and change in Western thought and its Eastern connections.* (Special issue of Sung Kyun Kwan Institute for Humanities.) Seoul: Sung Kyun Kwan University Press.

Canda, E. R., Shin, S., & Canda, H. (1993). Traditional philosophies of human service in Korea and contemporary social work implications. *Social Development Issues, 15*(3), 84-104.

Canda, E. R., & Canda, H. J. (1996). Korean spiritual philosophies of human service: Current state and prospects. *Social Development Issues, 18*(3), 53-70.

> This qualitative field study presents insights from Korean social work scholars about the applications of Buddhist, Confucian, Christian, and shamanistic ideas to contemporary social work. It is a follow-up to the Canda, Shin, and Canda (1993) study on Korean social welfare philosophies prior to 1900.

Furuto, S. M., Biswas, R., Chung, D. K., Murase, K., & Ross, S. (Eds.). (1992). *Social work practice with Asian Americans.* Newbury Park, CA: Sage.

Imbrogno, S., & Canda, E. (1988). Social work as an holistic system of activity. *Social Thought, 14*(1), 16-29.

Ryan, A. A. (1985). Cultural factors in casework with Chinese-Americans. *Social Casework, 66*(6), 333-340.

Sadeque, M. (1986). The survival characteristics of the poor: A case study of a village in Bangladesh. *Social Development Issues, 10*(1), 11-27.

Seplowin, V. M. (1992). Social work and karma therapy. *Spirituality and Social Work Journal, 3*(2), 2-8.

Singh, R. N. (1992). Integrating concepts from Eastern psychology and spirituality: A treatment approach for Asian-American clients. *Spirituality and Social Work Journal, 3*(2), 8-14.

> This article summarizes therapeutic concepts and techniques influenced by Asian spiritual disciplines, such as various yogas, biofeedback, and autogenic training. The author suggests applications of these to social work practice with Asian Americans and holistic social work in general.

Thangavelu, V. (1978). *Development of an Indian casework model: An ecological perspective.* Unpublished doctoral dissertation, Columbia University.

Timberlake, E. M., & Cook, K. O. (1984). Social work and the Vietnamese refugee. *Social Work, 29,* 108-114.

Titus, P. M. (1985). From charity to social work. *Indian Journal of Social Work, 46*(2), 157-166.

3. Hispanic, Latino/Latina (see also A.11)

Delgado, M. (1996). Religion as a caregiving system for Puerto Rican elders with functional disabilities. *Journal of Gerontological Social Work, 26*(3/4), 129-144.

> **This article reports the role of religious institutions in meeting the needs of Puerto Rican elders in New England. It is based on an empirical study of 558 people.**

Delgado, M., & Humm-Delgado, D. (1982). Natural support systems: Source of strength in Hispanic communities. *Social Work, 27,* 83-89.

> **The authors describe a variety of community-based social support systems prevalent in diverse Hispanic communities. These include traditional healing systems and religious institutions.**

Ghali, S. B. (1977). Culture sensitivity and the Puerto Rican client. *Social Casework, 59*(8), 459-468.

Ghali, S. B. (1985). *The recognition and use of Puerto Rican cultural values in treatment: A look at what is happening in the field and what can be learned from this.* Unpublished doctoral dissertation, New York University.

4. Indigenous/First Nations

Carter, I., & Parker, L. J. (1991). Intrafamilial sexual abuse in American Indian families. In M. Q. Patton (Ed.), *Family sexual abuse: Frontline research and evaluation* (pp. 106-117). Newbury Park, CA: Sage.

Chenault, V. (1990). A Native American practice framework. *Spirituality and Social Work Communicator, 1*(2), 5-7.

Coggins, K. (1990). *Alternative pathways to healing: The recovery medicine wheel.* Deerfield Beach, FL: Health Communications.

> **The author develops a holistic, 16-step process of recovery from addiction, tailored to indigenous people, by drawing on traditional medicine wheel teachings from various indigenous cultures.**

Cross, M. P. (1990). Holotropic breathwork and Native Americans. *Spirituality and Social Work Communicator, 1*(2), 11-12.

Cross, T. L. (1986). Drawing on cultural tradition in Indian child welfare practice. *Social Casework, 67*(5), 283-289.

DuBray, W. H. (1985). American Indian values: Critical factor in casework. *Social Casework, 66*(1), 30-37.

Horse, J. R. (1988). Cultural evolution of American Indian families. In C. Jacobs & D. D. Bowles (Eds.), *Ethnicity and race: Critical concepts in social work* (pp. 86-102). Silver Spring, MD: National Association of Social Workers.

Krill, D., & Pass, M. (1996). Sequential network therapy: Evolving a training model to treat alcoholism at an American Indian pueblo. *Reflections, 2*(2), 11-20.

Longclaws, L. (1989). Social work and the medicine wheel framework. In B. R. Compton & B. Galaway (Eds.), *Social work processes* (5th ed., pp. 25-33). Pacific Grove, CA: Brooks/Cole.

Mokuau, N. (1990). A family-centered approach in native Hawaiian culture. *Families in Society, 71*, 607-613.

> **Cultural and spiritual strengths of native Hawaiians are applied to develop a family and community-based approach to practice. This perspective was developed from interviews with five native Hawaiian healers who include connection with spiritual ancestors and gods in the helping process.**

Nabigon, H., & Mawhiney, A. (1996). Aboriginal theory: A Cree medicine wheel guide for healing First Nations. In F. J. Turner (Ed.), *Social work treatment: Interlocking theoretical approaches* (4th ed., pp. 18-38). New York: Free Press.

Stuart, P. (1981). The Christian church and Indian community life. *Journal of Ethnic Studies, 9*(3), 47-55.

Yellow Bird, M. J. (1995). Spirituality in First Nations story telling: A Sahnish-Hidatsa approach to narrative. *Reflections: Narratives of Professional Helping, 1*(4), 65-72.

> **The author presents principles that guide First Nations ways of story telling by giving illustrations from personal experience growing up in the Sahnish and Hidatsa communities. In this account, spirituality infuses daily life, messages delivered in oral traditions, and resilient responses to oppression.**

5. Other Cultural Issues

Canda, E. R. (1988). Religious aspects of transcultural relations: Value considerations for professional helpers. In D. B. Lee (Ed.), *Transcultural family process: Reflections and directions* (pp. 173-183). Columbus, OH: Transcultural Family Institute.

Cox, D. R. (1983). Religion and the welfare of immigrants. *Australian Social Work, 36*(1), 3-10.

Furman, L. E., & Chandy, J. M. (1998). Religion and spirituality: A long-neglected cultural component of rural social work practice. In L. H. Ginsberg (Ed.), *Social work in rural communities* (3rd ed., pp. 135-148). Alexandria, VA: Council on Social Work Education.

> **The authors report findings from a quantitative survey of social workers in a rural state about their perceptions of the importance of religion and spirituality in practice. Implications are given for including spirituality in culturally sensitive practice with rural populations.**

Graham, J. R., & Al-Krenawi, A. (1996). A comparison study of traditional helpers in a late nineteenth century Canadian (Christian) society in Toronto, Canada and in a late twentieth century Bedouin (Muslim) society in the Negev, Israel. *Journal of Multicultural Social Work, 4*(2), 31-45.

Lantz, J., & Pegram, M. (1989). Cross-cultural curative factors and clinical social work. *Journal of Independent Social Work, 4*(1), 55-68.

Lum, D. (1996). *Social work practice with people of color: A process stage approach* (3rd ed.). Pacific Grove, CA: Brooks/Cole.

Rey, L. D. (1997). Religion as invisible culture: Knowing about and knowing with. *Journal of Family Social Work, 2*(2), 159-177.

> **The author discusses the importance of including religious considerations in culturally competent family therapy. Four case examples are given pertaining to a wide range of religious and cultural backgrounds of family members.**

Tolliver, W. F. (1997). Invoking the spirit: A model for incorporating the spiritual dimension of human functioning into social work practice. *Smith College Studies in Social Work, 67*(3), 477-486.

C. Spirituality in Various Fields of Social Work

1. Addictions and Recovery (see also C.4 & C.6)

Carroll, M. M. (1993). Spiritual growth of recovering alcoholic adult children of alcoholics (Doctoral dissertation, University of Maryland at Baltimore). *University Microfilms International,* 9319831.

Gregoire, T. K. (1995). Alcoholism: The quest for transcendence and meaning. *Clinical Social Work Journal, 23*(3), 339-359.

> **The author argues that scientific understandings of alcoholism as a disease do not account for the profound existential issues involved. An approach to recovery that helps people find a new sense of meaning without alcohol is recommended.**

Krill, D. F. (1990). Reflections on teenage suicide and adult addictions. *Spirituality and Social Work Communicator, 1*(1), 10-11.

Master, L. (1989). Jewish experiences of Alcoholics Anonymous. *Smith College Studies in Social Work, 59*(2), 183-199.

Morell, C. (1996). Radicalizing recovery: Addiction, spirituality, and politics. *Social Work, 41,* 306-312.

> **This article proposes a way to bring individually focused treatment of addiction as a disease and spiritual issues together with radical commitment to empowerment and justice.**

Orth, L. W. (1988). *Women's patterns of spiritual healing in Alcoholics Anonymous: An exploratory study*. Unpublished master's thesis, Smith College.

Ronel, N. (1997). The universality of a self-help program of American origin: Narcotics anonymous in Israel. *Social Work in Health Care, 25*(3), 87-101.

Shore, J. (1978). The use of the self-identity workshop with recovering alcoholics. *Social Work with Groups, 1*(3), 299-307.

2. Aging (see also C.4 & C.5)

Filinson, R. (1988). A model for church-based services for frail elderly persons and their families. *The Gerontologist, 28*(4), 483-486.

Guy, R. F. (1982). Religion, physical disabilities and life satisfaction in older age cohorts. *International Journal of Aging and Human Development, 15*(3), 225-232.

Heisel, M. A., & Faulkner, A. O. (1982). Religiosity in an older Black population. *The Gerontologist, 22*(4), 354-358.

Menezes, L. (1990). A holistic approach to geriatric social work in a hospital setting (Doctoral dissertation, The Union Institute). *University Microfilms International,* 9107521.

Mindel, C. H., & Vaughan, C. C. (1978). A multidimensional approach to religiosity and disengagement. *Journal of Gerontology, 33*(1), 103-8.

Pieper, H. G. (1981). Church membership and participation in church activities among the elderly. *Activities, Adaptation and Aging, 1*(3), 23-29.

Seeber, J. J. (Ed.). (1990). Spiritual maturity in the later years [Special issue]. *Journal of Religious Gerontology, 7*(1/2).

> **This issue presents selected papers from a conference designed to develop a conceptual framework for understanding the connection between religion and aging. It draws on insights from theology, medicine, and psychotherapy.**

Studzinski, R. (1986). The religious challenges of aging. *Social Thought, 12*(3), 11-19.

Tobin, S. S., Ellor, J. W., & Anderson-Ray, S. (1986). *Enabling the elderly: Religious institutions within the service system*. Albany: State University of New York Press.

> **This interdisciplinary book discusses a holistic view of spiritual well-being, the nature of church- and synagogue-based programs for the elderly, findings from studies of four communities, and a model for effective interaction between religious and secular social service systems.**

3. Education

Alexander, L. B. (1983). The graduate school for Jewish social work, 1924–40: Training for social work in an ethnic community. *Journal of Education for Social Work, 19*(2), 5-15.

Amato-von Hemert, K., & Clark, J. (1994). Point/Counterpoint: Should social work education address religious issues? *Journal of Social Work Education, 30*, 7-17.

Blackman, D. V. (1983). Professor, I'm a Christian. *Social Work and Christianity, 10*(1), 74-84.

Canda, E. R. (1989). Religious content in social work education: A comparative approach. *Journal of Social Work Education, 25*, 36-45.

> **Insights from the field of comparative religious studies are used to develop a teaching methodology that addresses religious diversity within the context of social work values. Examples related to each component of the curriculum are given.**

Canda, E. R. (1997). Does religion and spirituality have a significant place in the core HBSE curriculum? Yes. In M. Bloom & W. C. Klein (Eds.), *Controversial issues in human behavior in the social environment* (pp. 172-177 and 183-184). Boston: Allyn and Bacon.

Cnaan, R. A., Goodfriend, T., & Newman, E. (1996). Jewish ethnic needs in multicultural social work education. *Journal of Teaching in Social Work, 13*(1/2), 157-168.

Cowley, A., & Derezotes, D. (1994). Transpersonal psychology and social work education. *Journal of Social Work Education, 30*, 32-41.

Derezotes, D. (1995). Spiritual and religious factors in practice: Empirically-based recommendations for social work education. *Arete, 20*(1), 1-15.

Dudley, J. R., & Helfgott, C. (1990). Exploring a place for spirituality in the social work curriculum. *Journal of Social Work Education, 26*, 287-294.

Fauri, D. P. (1988). Applying historical themes of the profession in the foundation curriculum. *Journal of Teaching in Social Work, 2*, 17-31.

Fulkerson, D. T. (1991). The perceived spirituality in traditional and nontraditional education: Implication for the social work curriculum (Master's thesis, California State University, Long Beach). *University Microfilms International,* 1344541.

Furman, L. E. (1994). Religion and spirituality in social work education: Preparing the culturally-sensitive practitioner for the future. *Social Work and Christianity, 21*(2), 103-117.

Heller, J. G. (1937). Common social objectives of religion, education, and social work. In *Proceedings of the National Conference of Social Workers* (pp. 284-294). Chicago: University of Chicago Press.

Herzog, S., & Russel, R. (1995). Spirituality courses in M.S.W. programs. *Society for Spirituality and Social Work Newsletter, 2*(2), 1-2.

Ifill, D. (1987). The role indoctrination plays in social work education. *Social Work and Christianity, 14*(2), 78-87.

> **The author critiques a tendency in social work education to discourage students from considering how to integrate faith into practice due to concern about indoctrinating clients. Four topics of potential indoctrination by educators themselves regarding diversity, spirituality, and values are discussed.**

Jarrett, H. H., & Howard, M. C. (1993). Chemical dependency content in CSWE-accredited BSW programs: A survey of course content and implications for further curricula development. *Human Services in the Rural Environment, 16*(4), 30-33.

Keith-Lucas, E. (1990). Some thoughts on undergraduate education for social work in Christian colleges. *Social Work and Christianity, 17*(1), 17-27.

Kuhlmann, E. G. (1984). Implications of CSWE nondiscrimination standards for baccalaureate social work programs in Christian colleges. *Social Work and Christianity, 11*(1), 3-15.

Marshall, J. (1991). The spiritual dimension in social work education. *Spirituality and Social Work Communicator, 2*(1), 12-14.

Netting, F. E., Thibault, J. M., & Ellor, J. W. (1990). Integrating content on organized religion into macropractice courses. *Journal of Social Work Education, 26*, 15-24.

The historical and contemporary significance of religious organizations in provision of social work and social welfare is discussed. The authors suggest macro practice content areas on religion to incorporate into courses on policy, organizations, and community.

Ortiz, L. P. A. (1991). Religious issues: The missing link in social work education. *Spirituality and Social Work Journal, 2*(2), 13-18.

Parr, R. G., & Jones, L. E. (1996). Point/Counterpoint: Should CSWE allow social work programs in religious institutions an exemption from the accreditation nondiscrimination standard related to sexual orientation? *Journal of Social Work Education, 32*, 297-313.

Two essays debate whether CSWE should allow religiously affiliated educational programs to have an exemption from the accreditation standard against discrimination on the basis of sexual orientation. Educational, ethical, and legal dilemmas and rival value positions are addressed.

Rice, D. S., & Dudley, J. R. (1997). Preparing students for the spiritual issues of their clients through a self-awareness exercise. *Journal of Baccalaureate Social Work, 3*(1), 85-95.

Russel, R. (1998). Spirituality and religion in graduate social work education. In E. R. Canda (Ed.), *Spirituality in social work: New directions* (pp. 15-29). Binghamton, NY: Haworth Pastoral Press.

Literature review and a survey of graduate programs of social work reveal current trends in content and teaching approaches regarding courses on spirituality and social work. Implications for educational innovation are identified.

Sheridan, M. J., Bullis, R. K., Adcock, C. R., Berlin, S. D., & Miller, P. C. (1992). Serving diverse religious client populations: Issues for education and practice. *Journal of Social Work Education, 28*, 190-203.

Sheridan, M. J., Wilmer, C. M., & Atcheson, L. (1994). Inclusion of content on religion and spirituality in the social work curriculum: A study of faculty views. *Journal of Social Work Education, 30*, 363-376.

> **The authors report findings from a survey of faculty at 25 schools of social work concerning their attitudes and practices about including content on spirituality and religion. Suggestions for educational innovation are offered.**

Simpkinson, C., Wengell, D., & Casavant, J. (Eds.). (1994). *The common boundary graduate education guide: Holistic programs and resources integrating spirituality and psychology.* Bethesda, MD: Common Boundary.

Soifer, S. (1991). Infusing content about Jews and about anti-semitism into the curricula. *Journal of Social Work Education, 27*, 156-67.

Spencer, S. W. (1961). What place has religion in social work education? *Social Service Review, 35*, 161-170.

Swaine, R. L., & Baird, V. (1977). An existentially based approach to teaching social work practice. *Journal of Education for Social Work, 13*(3), 98-106.

Van Soest, D. (1996). The influence of competing ideologies about homosexuality on nondiscrimination policy: Implications for social work education. *Journal of Social Work Education, 32*, 53-64.

Weisman, E. R. (1997). Does religion and spirituality have a significant place in the core HBSE curriculum? No. In M. Bloom & W. C. Klein (Eds.), *Controversial issues in human behavior in the social environment* (pp. 177-183). Boston: Allyn and Bacon.

4. Health and Physical Disability (see also C.1, C.2, & C.5)

Anderson, G. R. (1983). Medicine vs. religion: The case of Jehovah's Witnesses. *Health and Social Work, 8*(1), 31-38.

Dunbar, H. T., Mueller, C. W., Medina, C., & Wolf, T. (1998). Psychological and spiritual growth in women living with HIV. *Social Work, 43*, 144-154.

> **A qualitative study of 34 women living with HIV describes ways they were able to use their experience to support psychological and spiritual growth. The authors describe themes related to finding affirmation and meaning in understanding self, relationships, life, and death.**

George, I. (1990). AIDS and the Christian in social work. *Social Work and Christianity, 17*(2), 109-117.

Kahn, M. (1958). Some observations on the role of religion in illness. *Social Work, 3*(4), 83-89.

Kaplan, M. S., Marks, G., & Mertens, S. B. (1997). Distress and coping among women with HIV infection: Preliminary findings from a multiethnic sample. *American Journal of Orthopsychiatry, 67*(1), 80-91.

Rauch, J. B., & Kneen, K. K. (1989). Accepting the gift of life: Heart transplant recipients' post-operative adaptive tasks. *Social Work in Health Care, 14*(1), 47-59.

Rockowitz, R. J., Korpela, J. W., & Hunter, K. C. (1981). Social work dilemma: When religion and medicine clash. *Health and Social Work, 6*(4), 5-11.

Rosen, A., & Berry, K. (1978). Attribution of responsibility for marital sexual dysfunction and traditionalism. *Journal of Social Service Research, 1*(3), 287-97.

Ruffin, E. W. (1987). Values in social work ministry with families affected by mental retardation: A systems model. *Social Work and Christianity, 14*(2), 99-111.

Stern, R. C., Canda, E. R., & Doershuk, C. F. (1992). Use of non-medical treatment by cystic fibrosis patients. *Journal of Adolescent Health, 13,* 612-615.

Wallace, J. M., Jr., & Williams, D. R. (1997). Religion and adolescent health compromising behavior. In J. Schulenberg, J. L. Maggs, & K. Hurrelmann (Eds.), *Health risks and developmental transitions during adolescence* (pp. 444-468). New York: Cambridge University Press.

Weick, A. (1986). The philosophical context of a health model of social work. *Social Casework, 67*(9), 551-559.

Weinberg, N., & Sebian, C. (1980). The Bible and disability. *Rehabilitation Counseling Bulletin, 23*(4), 273-281.

York, G. Y. (1987). Religious-based denial in the NICU: Implications for social work. *Social Work in Health Care, 12*(4), 31-45.

> **This article describes harmful affects of religiously based denial by families of infants in intensive care. The responses of social workers and health teams to families' unrealistic hope for a miracle are presented.**

5. Loss and Death (see also C.2, C.4, & C.6)

Bagley, D., Ramsay, R. F. (1989). Attitudes toward suicide, religious values and suicidal behavior: Evidence from a community survey. In R. F. W. Diekstra, R. Maris, S. Platt, A. Schmidtke, & G. Sonneck (Eds.), *Suicide and its prevention: The role of attitude and imitation* (pp. 78-90). Leiden, Netherlands: Brill.

Chung, C. H. (1990). Death and dying: A Vietnamese cultural perspective. In J. K. Parry (Ed.), *Social work practice with the terminally ill: A transcultural perspective* (pp. 191-204). Springfield, IL: Thomas.

Early, B. P. (1998). Between two worlds: The psychospiritual crisis of a drying adolescent. In E. R. Canda (Ed.), *Spirituality in social work: New directions* (pp. 67-80). Binghamton, NY: Haworth Pastoral Press.

Easley, E. L. (1987). *The impact of traumatic events on religious faith: Implications for social work.* Unpublished doctoral dissertation, University of Alabama.

Fournier, R. R. (1990). Social work, spirituality and suicide: An odd mix or a natural blend? *Social Thought, 16*(3), 27-35.

Furn, B. G. (1987). Adjustment and the near-death experience: A conceptual and therapeutic model. *Journal of Near-Death Studies, 6*(1), 4-19.

Furn, B. G. (1987). Cross-cultural counseling and the near-death experience: Some elaborations. *Journal of Near-Death Studies, 6*(1), 37-40.

Greif, G. L., & Porembski, E. (1988). AIDS and significant others: Findings from a preliminary exploration of needs. *Health and Social Work, 13*(4), 259-265.

Hartman, P. M. (1996). *Finding meaning in crisis: A link between spirituality and social work practice.* Unpublished doctoral dissertation, University of Denver.

Ita, D. (1995-96). Testing of a causal model: Acceptance of death in hospice patients. *Omega: Journal of Death and Dying, 32*(2), 81-92.

Maneker, J. S., & Rankin, R. P. (1993). Religious homogamy and marital duration among those who file for divorce in California, 1966-1971. *Journal of Divorce and Remarriage, 19*(1/2), 233-247.

Millison, M., & Dudley, J. (1990). The importance of spirituality in hospice work. *The Hospice Journal, 6*(3), 63.

Moynihan, R., Christ, G., & Silver, L. G. (1988). AIDS and terminal illness. *Social Casework, 69*(6), 380-387.

Nakashima, M. (1995). Spiritual growth through hospice social work. *Reflections: Narratives of Professional Helping, 1*(4), 17-27.

> **A hospice social worker describes how Japanese culture and religious traditions, together with social work training in the United States, influence her way of relating to dying and death. Personal insights into hospice practice are recounted.**

Nathanson, I. G. (1995). Divorce and women's spirituality. *Journal of Divorce and Remarriage, 22*(3/4), 179-188.

Paulino, A. M. (1995a). Death, dying, and religion among Dominican immigrants. In J. Parry & A. R. Shen (Eds.), *A cross-cultural look at death, dying, and religion* (pp. 84-101). Chicago: Nelson-Hall.

Reese, D., & Brown, D. (1997). Psychosocial and spiritual care in hospice: Differences between nursing, social work, and clergy. *Hospice Journal, 12*(1), 29-41.

Roy, A. (1991). The Book of Job: A grief and human development interpretation. *Journal of Religion and Health, 30*(2), 149-159.

Smith, E. D. (1995). Addressing the psychospiritual distress of death as reality: A transpersonal approach. *Social Work, 40*, 402-412.

> **The author uses insights from transpersonal theory, especially Ken Wilber, to formulate a transegoic model of development. This model describes how people**

can work toward a sense of meaning and transcendence by confronting issues of mortality.

Smith, E. D., & Gray, C. (1995). Integrating and transcending divorce: A transpersonal model. *Social Thought, 18*(1), 57-74.

Smith, E. D., Stefanek, M. E., Joseph, M. V., & Verdieck, M. J. (1993). Spiritual awareness, personal perspective on death and psychosocial distress among cancer patients: An initial investigation. *Journal of Psychosocial Oncology, 11*(3), 89-103.

Sormanti, M., & August, J. (1997). Parental bereavement: Spiritual connections with deceased children. *American Journal of Orthopsychiatry, 67*(3), 461-470.

> **A study of 43 bereaved parents of children with cancer describes a common sense of parents' connection with their deceased child. Implications for research and practice are presented.**

Weinberg, N. (1995). Does apologizing help? The role of self blame and making amends in recovery from bereavement. *Health and Social Work, 20*(4), 294-299.

6. Mental Health, Psychotherapy, and Micro Practice

Becvar, D. S. (1997). *Soul healing: A spiritual orientation in counseling and therapy.* New York: Basic Books.

Becvar, D. S. (Ed.). (1998). *Family, spirituality and social work.* Binghamton, NY: Haworth.

> **This collection discusses spirituality in relation to mental health and clinical social work, including case studies and concepts of spirituality. Insights from social constructionism, women's issues, and the relational systems model are presented.**

Bilodeau, F. (1979). Le travail social et Wilhelm Reich. *Canadian Journal of Social Work Education, 5*(2&3), 76-88.

Brothers, B. (Ed.). (1993). *Spirituality and couples: Heart and soul in the therapy process.* Binghamton, NY: Haworth.

> **This collection integrates spirituality into psychotherapy with couples. It includes insights from Satir's family therapy, Buddhist meditation, and the Jewish theme of exile, yearning, and return.**

Bullis, R. K. T. (1993). Religious/spiritual factors in clinical social work practice: An examination of assessment, intervention and ethics (Doctoral dissertation, Virginia Commonwealth University). *University Microfilms International,* 9417614.

Cadwallander, E. H. (Ed.). (1991). Depression and religion. *Counseling and Values, 35*(2), entire issue.

Canda, E. R. (1988). Therapeutic transformation in ritual, therapy, and human development. *Journal of Religion and Health, 27*(3), 205-220.

Cornett, C. (1998). *The soul of psychotherapy: Recapturing the spiritual dimension in the therapeutic encounter*. New York: Free Press.

> **This book provides many stories from psychotherapy practice that illustrate the helpful and harmful influences of religion and spirituality on clients. Using a perspective strongly influenced by psychoanalysis, the author offers suggestions and examples for therapeutic response to these influences.**

Cornett, C. (1992). Toward a more comprehensive personology: Integrating a spiritual perspective into social work practice. *Social Work, 37*, 101-102.

Danylchuk, L. S. (1992). The pastoral counselor as mental health professional: A comparison of the training of AAPC fellow pastoral counselors and licensed clinical social workers. *Journal of Pastoral Care, 46*(4), 382-391.

Derezotes, D. S. (1995). Spirituality and religiosity: Neglected factors in social work practice. *Arete, 20*(1), 1-15.

DiBlasio, F. A., & Proctor, J. H. (1993). Therapists and the clinical use of forgiveness. *American Journal of Family Therapy, 21*(2), 175-184.

DiBlasio, F. A. (1993). The role of social workers' religious beliefs in helping family members forgive. *Families in Society, 74*(3), 167-170.

> **A quantitative study of social workers who are certified as marriage and family therapists examines attitudes and practices regarding forgiveness. Literature review and case description amplify recommendations for increased use of forgiveness-related therapeutic practices.**

Dixon, S. L., & Sands, R. G. (1983). Identity and the experience of crisis. *Social Casework, 64*(4), 223-230.

Ferranti, J. (1996). Social work and past life regression therapy. *Society for Spirituality and Social Work Newsletter, 3*(2), 3, 10.

Goldberg, C. (1996). The privileged position of religion in the clinical dialogue. *Clinical Social Work Journal, 24*(2), 125-136.

Haake, L. (1996). *Love made visible: A qualitative study of spiritually oriented clinical social work practice*. Unpublished master's thesis, Catholic University of America.

Hammond, R. A. (1991). Conceptualizing the place of spirituality in psychotherapy: Implications for professional education (Doctoral dissertation, Case Western Reserve University). *University Microfilms International*, 3538-3539.

Horowitz, R. (1991). Reflections on the casework relationship: Beyond empiricism. *Health and Social Work, 16*(3), 170-175.

Iorfido, B. (1996). Incorporating faith into the recovery model for a person with multiple personality disorder. *Social Work and Christianity, 23*(2), 87-101.

Jaffe, M. S. (1961). Opinions of caseworkers about religious issues in practice. *Smith College Studies in Social Work, 31*(3), 238-256.

Joseph, M. V. (1987). The religious and spiritual aspects of clinical practice: A neglected dimension of social work. *Social Thought, 13*(1), 12-23.

Joseph, M. V. (1988). Religion and social work practice. *Social Casework, 69*(7), 443-452.

> **This article reports an exploratory and descriptive survey of 61 clinical social workers at a church-related social work program regarding their attitudes about religion in practice. The author advocates for greater attention to religious and spiritual issues in social work practice.**

Kaiser-Ryan, V. T. (1991). *Concept of God: The relationship to depression in psychiatric patients.* Unpublished doctoral dissertation, Fordham University.

Keefe, T. (1975). Meditation and the psychotherapist. *American Journal of Orthopsychiatry, 45*(3), 484-489.

Keefe, T. (1996). Meditation and social work treatment. In F. J. Turner (Ed.), *Social work treatment: Interlocking theoretical approaches* (4th ed., pp. 434-460). New York: Free Press.

> **The author provides an introduction to research, theory, and techniques concerning therapeutic uses of various types of meditation, especially those influenced by Zen. Suggestions and a case example are given for the incorporation of meditation into clinical practice.**

Kilpatrick, A. C., & Holland, T. P. (1990). Spiritual dimensions of practice. *Clinical Supervisor, 8*(2), 125-140.

Liebenberg, B. (1983). The group therapist and the patient: Countertransference and resistance in group psychotherapy. *Smith College Studies in Social Work, 53*(2), 85-102.

Logan, S. L. (1997). Meditation as a tool for linking the personal and professional. *Reflections: Narratives of Professional Helping, 3*(1), 38-44.

Luoma, B. (1998). An exploration of intuition for social work practice and education. In E. R. Canda (Ed.), *Spirituality in social work: New directions* (pp. 31-45). Binghamton, NY: Haworth Pastoral Press.

Nakhaima, J. M. (1994). Network family counseling: The overlooked resource. *Arete, 19*(1), 46-56.

Nakhaima, J. M., & Dicks, B. H. (1995). Social work practice with religious families. *Families in Society, 76*(6), 360-368.

Pezzulo, D. J. (1997). *Social workers' clinical decisions regarding religious and spiritual issues in direct practice: A quantitative analysis.* Unpublished doctoral dissertation, University of Pittsburgh.

Raider, M. C. (1992). Assessing the role of religion in family functioning. In L. A. Burton (Ed.), *Religion and the family: When God helps* (pp. 165-183). Binghamton, NY: Haworth Pastoral Press.

Roitman, R. (1996). Depression and lack of faith. *Society for Spirituality and Social Work Newslettter, 3*(1), 2-3.

Sands, R. G. (1983). The DSM-III and psychiatric nosology: A critique from the labeling perspective. *California Sociologist, 6*(1), 77-87.

Satir, V. (1988). *The new people making.* Mountain View, CA: Science and Behavior Books.

A social worker who was one of the most influential contributors to the development of family therapy describes her approach to practice in detail. The author employs a creative and holistic approach to families, with explicit attention to spiritual aspects of people.

Schatz, M. S., & Horejsi, C. (1996). The importance of religious tolerance: A module for educating foster parents. *Child Welfare, 75,* 73-86.

Sermabeikian, P. (1994). Our clients, ourselves: The spiritual perspective and social work practice. *Social Work, 39,* 178-183.

Sheridan, M. J. (1995). Honoring angels in my path: Spiritually-sensitive group work with persons who are incarcerated. *Reflections: Narratives of Professional Helping, 1*(4), 5-16.

Simons, B. (1992). Acknowledging spirituality in recovery: A mental health consumer's perspective. *Spirituality and Social Work Journal, 3*(1), 5-7.

Small, J. (1982). *Transformers: The therapists of the future.* Marina del Rey, CA: DeVores.

Spero, M. H. (1987). Current trends in psychotherapy, clinical social work, and religious values: A review and bibliography. *Journal of Social Work and Policy in Israel, 2,* 81-110.

Spero, M. H. (1987). Identity and individuality in the nouveau-religious patient: Theoretical and clinical aspects. *Journal of Social Work and Policy in Israel, 1,* 25-49.

Sullivan, W. P. (1992). Spirituality as social support for individuals with severe mental illness. *Spirituality and Social Work Journal, 3*(1), 7-13.

Titone, A. M. (1991). A spirituality and personal growth seminar for clients. *Spirituality and Social Work Journal, 2*(2), 10-13.

Titone, A. M. (1991). Spirituality and psychotherapy in social work practice. *Spirituality and Social Work Journal, 2*(1), 7-9.

Walsh, J. (1995). The impact of schizophrenia on clients' religious beliefs: Implications for families. *Families in Society, 76*(9), 551-558.

Wetzel, J. (1984). *Clinical handbook of depression.* New York: Gardner.

The author provides a broad overview of various approaches to theory and treatment of depression. A holistic framework, including spirituality, is given to integrate insights from these approaches. Special attention is given to insights from feminism and existentialism.

7. Policy, Law, and Macro Practice

Buhner, S. (1992). Controversies in the regulation of spiritually oriented helping. *Spirituality and Social Work Journal, 3*(1), 18-23.

Bullis, R. K. (1991). The spiritual healing "defense" as applied in criminal prosecutions for crimes against children. *Child Welfare, 70,* 541-555.

Bullis, R. K., & Harrigan, M. (1992). Religious denominational policies on sexuality: Implications for social work practice. *Families in Society, 73*(5), 304-312.

> **Policies on sexual issues from several denominations are discussed in relation to social work practice. Suggestions are given for ethical consideration of religious and spiritual issues of clients concerning sexuality.**

Canda, E., Chambers, D., & Sullivan, P. (1993). Should spiritual principles guide social policy? In H. J. Karger & J. Midgley (Eds.), *Controversial issues in social policy* (pp. 63-78). Boston: Allyn and Bacon.

> **Two sets of authors debate whether spirituality and religion should be included explicitly in social policy formation. The dangers of sectarian rivalry and moralistic agendas are considered along with constructive ways to include values, morality, and spiritual perspectives in policy-making processes.**

Day, P. J. (1980). *A new history of social welfare.* Englewood Cliffs, NJ: Prentice Hall.

Evans, E. N. (1985). Influencing decision-making in public policy: Religious organizations and political process. *Social Work and Christianity, 12*(1), 26-37.

Freedberg, S. (1986). Religion, profession, and politics: Bertha Capen Reynolds' challenge to social work. *Smith College Studies in Social Work, 56*(2), 95-110.

McLauglin, C., & Davidson, G. (1994). *Spiritual politics.* New York: Ballantine.

> **This book provides a holistic worldview as a basis for social action and political activity. Numerous social activist movements and political organizations are described that explicitly include an approach to spirituality respecting diversity and mutual benefit of all people.**

Midgely, J., & Sanzenbach, P. (1989). Social work, religion, and the global challenge of fundamentalism. *International Social Work, 32*(4), 273-287.

Netting, F. E. (1984). The changing environment: Its effect on church related agencies. *Social Work and Christianity, 11*(1), 16-30.

Ressler, L. B. (1998). The relation between church and state: Issues in social work and the law. In E. R. Canda (Ed.), *Spirituality in social work: New directions* (pp. 81-95). Binghamton, NY: Haworth Pastoral Press.

Smith, E. P. (1995). Willingness and resistance to change: The case of the Race Discrimination Amendment of 1942. *Social Service Review, 69,* 31-56.

Sullivan, P. (1994). Should spiritual principles guide social policy? No. In H. J. Karger & J. Midgley (Eds.), *Controversial issues in human behavior in the social environment* (pp. 69-74). Boston: Allyn and Bacon.

Vandezande, G. (1997). Public justice through confessional pluralism: Towards reconciliation in a divided world. *Social Work and Christianity, 24*(1), 2-18.

Walz, T., & Canda. E. (1988). Gross national consumption in the United States: Implications for Third World development. *International Journal of Contemporary Sociology, 25*(3), 165-175.

Weber, P. J., & Jones, W. L. (1994). *U.S. religious interest groups: Institutional profiles.* Westport, CT: Greenwood.

Westby, O. (1985). Religious groups and institutions. In G. A. Tobin (Ed.), *Social planning and human service delivery in the voluntary sector* (pp. 47-73). Westport, CT: Greenwood.

Wuthnow, R., & Hodgkinson, V. A. (1990). *Faith and philanthropy in America: Exploring the role of religion in America's voluntary sector.* San Francisco: Jossey-Bass.

D. General Concepts, Concerns, and Approaches about Spirituality and Religion

Barker, R. L. (1999). *The social work dictionary* (4th ed.). Washington, DC: NASW Press.

Benda, B. B. (n. d.). The effect of religion on adolescent delinquency revisited. *Journal of Research in Crime and Delinquency, 32*(4), 446-466.

Benda, B. B., & Corwyn, R. F. (1997). A test of a model with reciprocal effects between religiosity and various forms of delinquency using 2 stage least squares regression. *Journal of Social Service Research, 22*(3), 27-52.

Brower, I. C. (1984). The 4th ear of the spiritual-sensitive social worker. (Doctoral dissertation, Union for Experimenting Colleges and Universities, 1984). *University Microfilms International*, 8500785.

Bullis, R. K. (1996). *Spirituality in social work practice.* Washington, DC: Taylor and Francis.

> **This book offers a paradigm and suggestions for addressing spirituality in both micro and macro practice. Issues of religious and cultural diversity are addressed. Findings from regional surveys of social workers' use of spiritual helping activities are presented.**

Cabot, R. C. (1927). The inter-relation of social work and the spiritual life. *The Family, 8*(7), 211-217.

Canda, E. R. (1986). A conceptualization of spirituality for social work: Its issues and implications (Doctoral dissertation, Ohio State University). *University Microfilms International*, 8625190.

Canda, E. R. (1988). Conceptualizing spirituality for social work: Insights from diverse perspectives. *Social Thought, 14*(1), 30-46.

Canda, E. R. (1988). Spirituality, religious diversity, and social work practice. *Social Casework, 69*(4), 238-247.

Canda, E. R. (1989). Religion and social work: A response to Sanzenbach. *Social Casework, 70*(9), 572-574.

Canda, E. R. (1990). Afterword: Spirituality re-examined. *Spirituality and Social Work Communicator, 1*(1), 13-14.

Canda, E. R. (1995). Retrieving the soul of social work. *Society for Spirituality and Social Work Newsletter, 2*(2), 5-8.

Canda, E. R. (Ed.). (1995). Spirituality: A special issue. *Reflections: Narratives of Professional Helping 1*(4).

Canda, E. R. (1997). Spirituality. In R. L. Edwards (Ed.-in-Chief), *Encyclopedia of social work* (19th ed., Suppl., pp. 299-309). Washington, DC: NASW Press.

Canda, E. R. (Ed.). (1998). *Spirituality in social work: New directions.* Binghamton, NY: Haworth Pastoral Press.

> This collection describes and advocates for innovations in relation to conceptualization of spirituality and religion, social work education, spiritually sensitive clinical practice, legal concerns regarding church/state separation, and re-envisioning basic principles guiding the social work profession.

Canda, E. R., & Furman, L. D. (1999). *Spiritual diversity in social work practice: The heart of helping.* New York: Free Press.

> The authors provide a practice framework of values and ethics, knowledge about diverse spiritual perspectives, and practice application of spiritually sensitive social work. Exercises encourage personal and professional growth. Examples are given from a national survey of NASW members and stories of personal and professional experience.

Carroll, M. M. (1998). Social work's conceptualization of spirituality. In E. R. Canda (Ed.), *Spirituality in social work: New Directions* (pp. 1-13). Binghamton, NY: Haworth Pastoral Press.

Coles, R. (1993). *The call of service.* Boston: Houghton Mifflin.

Constable, R. (1990). Spirituality and social work: Issues to be addressed. *Spirituality and Social Work Communicator, 1*(1), 4-6.

Corbett, L. (1925). Spiritual factors in case work. *The Family, 6*(8), 223-227.

Cowley, A. S. (1996). Expressing the soul of social work. *Society for Spirituality and Social Work Newsletter, 3*(2), 1, 6-8.

Cox, D. (1985). The missing dimension in social work practice. *Australian Social Work, 36*(4), 5-11.

Dass, R., & Gorman, P. (1985). *How can I help?* New York: Knopf.

> The authors use numerous stories and philosophical reflections from professional helpers, volunteers, and various religious traditions to illustrate the central role of compassion and spiritual awareness in service.

Derezotes, D. (1996). Spiritual materialism and social work. *Society for Spirituality and Social Work Newsletter, 3*(1), 4.

Derezotes, D. S., & Evans, K. E. (1995). Spirituality and religiosity in practice: In-depth interviews of social work practitioners. *Social Thought, 18*(1), 39-56.

> **Interviews of 56 social workers in Utah revealed distinctions between religion and spirituality, a summary of practice interests, and suggestions for increased training.**

Faver, C. A. (1986). Religion, research, and social work. *Social Thought, 12*(3), 20-29.

Foehrenbach, A. J. (1957). Religion and social work. *Social Work, 2,* 73-74.

Goldstein, H. (1990). The knowledge base of social work practice: Theory, wisdom, analogue, or art? *Families in Society, 71*(1), 32-43.

Gustafson, J. M . (1982). Professions as "callings." *Social Service Review, 56,* 501-515.

Haworth, G. O. (1984). Social work research, practice, and paradigms. *Social Service Review, 58,* 343-357.

Ikenberry, J. (1975). Psi and our cosmic age. *Clinical Social Work Journal, 3*(4), 316-330.

Johnson, F. E. (1956). *Religion and social work.* New York: Institute for Religious and Social Studies, Harper and Brothers.

Johnson, S. K. (1997). Does spirituality have a place in rural social work? *Social Work and Christianity, 24*(1), 58-66.

Johnstone, B. V. (1986). The theory and strategy of the seamless garment. *Social Thought, 12*(4), 19-27.

Loewenberg, F. M. (1988). *Religion and social work practice in contemporary American society.* New York: Columbia University Press.

> **This was the first book to address a wide range of religious issues in contemporary social work practice. Most examples relate to Christian and Jewish forms of religiosity. The author promotes a nonsectarian approach that respects both religious commitments and social work ethics.**

Logan, S. L. (1990). Critical issues in operationalizing the spiritual dimension of social work practice. *Spirituality and Social Work Communicator, 1*(1), 7-9.

Marty, M. E. (1980). Social service: Godly and godless. *Social Service Review, 54,* 463-481.

Meinert, R. G., Pardeck, J. T., & Murphy, J. W. (Eds.). (1998). *Postmodernism, religion, and the future of social work.* Binghamton, NY: Haworth Pastoral Press.

Meystedt, D. M. (1984). Religion and the rural population: Implications for social work. *Social Casework, 65*(4), 219-226.

Middleman, R., & Wood, G. (1991). Seeing/believing/seeing. *Social Work, 36,* 243-246.

Midgley, J., & Sanzenbach, P. (1989). Social work, religion, and the global challenge of Fundamentalism. *International Social Work, 32*(4), 273-287.

Nelson, M. C. (1975). Psi in the family. *Clinical Social Work Journal, 3*(4), 279-285.

O'Brien, P. J. (1992). Social work and spirituality: Clarifying the concept for practice. *Spirituality and Social Work Journal, 3*(1), 2-5.

Ragg, N. M. (1977). *People, not cases: A philosophical approach to social work.* London: Routledge and Kegan Paul.

Raines, J. (1996). Toward a definition of spiritually-sensitive social work practice. *Society for Spirituality and Social Work Newsletter, 3*(2), 4-5.

Robbins, S. P., Canda, E. R., & Chatterjee, P. (1998). *Contemporary human behavior theory: A critical perspective for social work.* Boston: Allyn and Bacon.

> The authors give detailed summaries and critiques of major schools of human behavior theory, including transpersonal, as applied to social work. Spirituality is addressed in presentation of every theory and in a holistic approach to using theory in micro and macro practice.

Sanzenbach, P. (1989). Religion and social work: It's not that simple. *Social Casework, 70*(9), 571-572.

Sermabeikian, P. (1994). Our clients, ourselves: The spiritual perspective and social work practice. *Social Work, 39*, 178-183.

Sheridan, M. J. (1997). If we nurtured the soul of social work. *Society for Spirituality and Social Work Newsletter, 4*(2), 3.

Sheridan, M. J., & Bullis, R. K. (1991). Practitioners' views on religion and spirituality: A qualitative study. *Spirituality and Social Work Journal, 2*(2), 2-10.

Siporin, M. (1985). Current social work perspectives on clinical practice. *Clinical Social Work Journal, 13*(3), 198-217.

Siporin, M. (1990). Welcome to the Spirituality and Social Work Communicator. *Spirituality and Social Work Communicator, 1*(1), 3-4.

Spencer, S. (1956). Religion and social work. *Social Work, 1*(3), 19-26.

Stroup, H. (1962). The common predicament of religion and social work. *Social Work, 7*(2), 89-93.

Taft, J. (1994). The spirit of social work. *Families in Society, 74*, 243-248. (Reprinted from 1928.)

Towle, C. (1965). *Common human needs* (rev. ed.). Washington, DC: National Association of Social Workers.

> This reissue of an influential book advocates for social workers to address physical, mental, social, and spiritual needs, especially in the context of social welfare systems. The original (1945) was an early presentation of a bio-psycho-social-spiritual model of the person in environment.

Weick, A. (1987). Reconceptualizing the philosophical perspective of social work. *Social Service Review, 61*, 218-230.

E. Ethics, Values, and Moral Issues

Ashford, S., & Timms, N. (1990). Values in social work: Investigations of the practice of family placement. *British Journal of Social Work, 20*(1), 1-20.

Berrick, J. D. (1991). Welfare and child care: The intricacies of competing social values. *Social Work, 36*, 345-351.

Black, P. N., Hartley, E. K., Whelley, J., & Kirk-Sharp, C. (1989). Ethics curricula: A national survey of graduate schools of social work. *Social Thought, 15*, 141-148.

Brown, C. (1989). Reflections on the role of personal values in guiding social work practice: Where values and actions meet. *Social Work and Christianity, 16*(2), 71-85.

Bullis, R. K. (1995). *Clinical social worker misconduct.* Chicago: Nelson-Hall.

Canda, E. R. (1990). Spiritual diversity and social work values. In J. J. Kattakayam (Ed.), *Contemporary social issues* (pp. 1-20). Trivandrum, India: University of Kerala.

Canda, E. R., & Yellow Bird, M. J. (1996). Cross-tradition borrowing of spiritual practices in social work settings. *Society for Spirituality and Social Work Newsletter, 3*(1), 1, 7.

Conrad, A. P. (1988). Ethical considerations in the psychosocial process. *Social Casework, 71*, 603-610.

Conrad, A. P. (1989). Developing an ethics review process in a social service agency. *Social Thought, 15*, 102-115.

Constable, R. T. (1983). Values, religion, and social work practice. *Social Thought, 9*(4), 29-41.

> **The religious roots of professional social work values are explored in relation to three general goals: social justice, freedom, and relational love.**

Elliott, M. W. (1984). *Ethical issues in social work: An annotated bibliography.* New York: Council on Social Work Education.

Faver, C. A. (1986). Belief systems, social work, and social change. *Journal of Applied Social Sciences, 10*(2), 119-131.

> **The relationship between religious and nonreligious belief systems and social work is discussed in regard to both theory and empirical research approaches. The role of images of God and humankind is emphasized.**

Faver, C. A. (1987). Religious beliefs, professional values, and social work. *Journal of Applied Social Sciences, 11*(2), 206-219.

Goldstein, H. (1987). The neglected moral link in social work practice. *Social Work, 32*, 181-186.

Holland, T. P. (1989). Values, faith, and professional practice. *Social Thought, 15*(1), 28-40.

Hughes, J. (1984). Toward a moral philosophy for social work. *Social Thought, 10*, 3-17.

Imre, R. W. (1989). Moral theory for social work. *Social Thought, 15*(1), 18-27.

Kreutziger, S. S. (1991). *Going on to perfection: The contributions of the Wesleyan theological doctrine of entire sanctification to the value base of American professional social work through the lives and activities of nineteenth-century evangelical women reformers.* Unpublished doctoral dissertation, Tulane University.

Joseph, M. V. (1985). A model for ethical decision making in clinical practice. In C. B. Germain (Ed.), *Advances in clinical practice* (pp. 207-217). Silver Spring, MD: National Association of Social Workers.

Joseph, M. V. (1989). Social work ethics: Historical and contemporary perspectives, *Social Thought, 15*, 4-17.

Joseph, M. V., & Conrad, A. P. (1989). Social work influence on interdisciplinary ethical decision making in health care settings. *Health and Social Work, 14*(2), 22-30.

Leiby, J. (1985). Moral foundations of social welfare and social work: A historical view. *Social Work, 30*, 323-330.

> **The author discusses three moral justifications for social welfare in American history: charity (in religious and secular forms), constitutional "police power," and responsibility of the state to protect the community.**

Levy, C. S. (1976). *Social work ethics*. New York: Human Sciences Press.

Loewenberg, F., & Dolgoff, R. (1992). *Ethical decisions for social work practice* (4th ed.). Itasca, IL: Peacock.

McCann, C. W., & Cutler, J. P. (1979). Ethics and the alleged unethical. *Social Work, 24*, 5-8.

Morehouse, M., & Skarsten, S. (1983). Ethics and psychotherapy. *Social Work and Christianity, 10*(2), 6-21.

National Association of Social Workers. (1996). *NASW Code of Ethics*. Washington, DC: Author.

Poppendieck, J. E. (1992). Values, commitments, and ethics of social work in the United States. *Journal of Progressive Human services, 3*(2), 31-45.

Pumphrey, M. W. (1961). Transmitting values and ethics through social work practice. *Social Work, 6*(3), 68-75.

Reamer, F. G. (1987). Ethics committees in social work. *Social Work, 32*, 188-192.

Reamer, F. G. (1987). Values and ethics. In A. Minahan et al. (Eds.), *Encyclopedia of social work* (pp. 801-809). Silver Spring, MD: National Association of Social Workers.

Reamer, F. G. (1990). *Ethical dilemmas in social service* (2nd ed.). New York: Columbia University Press.

Reamer, F. G. (1995). Ethics consultation in social work. *Social Thought, 18*(1), 3-16.

Reamer, F. G., & Abramson, M. (1982). *The teaching of social work ethics.* Hastings-on-Hudson, NY: Hastings Center.

Reid, P. N., & Popple, P. R. (Eds.). (1992). *The moral purposes of social work: The character and intentions of a profession.* Chicago: Nelson-Hall.

> This collection of essays presents historical and contemporary moral dilemmas and debates concerning social control and social justice. Various chapters discuss the role of religiously based principles.

Rhodes, M. (1986). *Ethical dilemmas in social work practice.* London: Routledge and Kegan Paul.

Roberts, C. S. (1989). Conflicting professional values in social work and medicine. *Health and Social Work, 14*(3), 211-218.

Siporin, M. (1982). Moral philosophy in social work today. *Social Service Review, 56,* 516-538.

Siporin, M. (1983). Morality and immorality in working with clients. *Social Thought, 9*(4), 10-27.

Siporin, M. (1986). Contribution of religious values to social work and the law. *Social Thought, 12,* 40-41.

> The author discusses problems in social work and the legal profession resulting from loss of religiously based values during secularization. A return to religious insights about values and morality is encouraged.

Spencer, S. W. (1957). Religious and spiritual values in social casework practice. *Social Casework, 57,* 519-526.

> Judeo-Christian religious values influencing casework are discussed. The author advocates for a nonsectarian application of these values to address spiritual aspects of clients.

Worthington, E. L., Jr. (1988). Understanding the values of religious clients: A model and its application to counseling. *Journal of Counseling Psychology, 35*(2), 166-174.